"I believe every human should get a copy of th  has done a truly amazing job. It is a wonderfu

— Manyu, internationally reno\

"This book has a clear vision of teaching us the path to true happiness ... ... mind, soul and spirit. It is a wonderful read and I will come back to dip in its waters many, many times."

— Dan John, strength coaching legend, religious studies academic, best-selling author of eleven books including *Never Let Go*

"200% holds so much real life relatable wisdom. I know this book will change lives because it makes living the best of lives possible for anyone with an inner desire and calling for more. If 'more' is calling you, then Arjuna's book is the answer."

— Sandy C. Newbigging, coaching and meditation expert, best-selling author of seven books including *Mind Detox*

"200% is written with such clarity and humour that simply reading it is an enormous pleasure. But it doesn't stop there – if readers put these words into action there will be a tremendous impact, not just on themselves, but on the entire world."

— Rebekah Palmer, journalist, editor, author of two books including *Rhythm*, as well as the children's series *Champ the Chopper*

"Arjuna strikes that just right balance between finding inner peace and living to perform. These two aspects, commonly at odds, need no longer be. Welcome to the 200% club."

— Pat Flynn, fitness expert, philosopher, best-selling author of five books including *How to Be Better at (Almost) Everything*, top 500 health and fitness blogger

"I absolutely LOVE it. I love the mixture of wisdom, humility and humour. I love the format and the very real and practical advice, which is life changing. Everyone should read this book!"

— Joanna Taylor, international yoga and meditation expert

200%

An Instruction Manual for Living Fully

Arjuna Ishaya

200% – An Instruction Manual for Living Fully

Cover design, illustration and photography by Ali Hodgson, www.alihodgson.co.uk

Visit www.arjunaishaya.com

Paperback ISBN: 978-0-9572056-7-3
eBook ISBN: 978-0-9572056-8-0

Thread of Souls Publishing

To my fellow Ishayas, you who are dedicated to living the greatest of lives. You've always been an inspiration and a beacon of hope to me; may all those who want the greatest of lives find you.

To Sumati and May, you *are* the greatest – thank you for being part of my life.

"Be Whole Assed."

- Maharishi Krishnananda Ishaya,
  Bright Path Ishaya teacher

CONTENTS

ACKNOWLEDGEMENTS

"Nothing of me is original.
I am the combined effort of everybody I have ever known."

- Chuck Palahniuk, author of *The Fight Club*

If you have ever worked closely with a great teacher, mentor or coach, you will know how much you hold this person in the greatest esteem and respect.

Everything in this book is due to my Bright Path Ishaya teacher, Maharishi Krishnananda Ishaya. I have taken his teachings, placed my peculiar filter over the top, and presented you with the results.

He always says you get the teacher you deserve, and I feel incredibly fortunate. If indeed there is such a thing as previous lives, I must have done something very, very right. Thank you Maharishi, for everything.

Thank you, from the bottom of my heart, to Savitri and Prasada for such brilliant work editing and all the amazing support. You guys went far beyond the call of duty, I am forever in your debt. To Kali for the incredible cover, all the design work and advice. You are so cool and so talented. To Sandy for the beautiful foreword. To Sutratman for putting this all in such a perfect order and everything else you do. You're an inspiration. To Dharani for all your editing work, that helped so much. To

Julian, for a sensational job with all your comments and proof-reading. To Purya for such a phenomenal job – you are awesome. And to Tapas, wow! Thank you.

And thank *you* – for taking the time to read this. May you always live 200% of life.

Is There More To Life Than This?

"There is more to life than increasing its speed."

- Mahatma Gandhi, Indian political and spiritual leader

Are you way too happy? Do you suffer from problematically high levels of inner peace? Or are you tired of loving your life too much? I don't know anyone that is *too* happy, *too* peaceful or *too* in love with their life. I believe this is because there is always more available to us, and something, somewhere inside us, knows it.

"There must be more to life than this." Have you ever thought or felt the sentiments of this sentence? There is a very high chance that you have, especially if you've been drawn to this book. Feeling that *there must be more to life than this* is so common because, in reality, there *is* so much more than what the average person experiences, and again some part of us knows it all too well.

The average human life goes something like this: Get born, learn the basics (how to walk, talk, eat etc.), go to school (learn how to count, write, think etc.), leave school, do things to earn money, go places, find a mate, get married, have kids, buy a house, buy more stuff, work 30-40 years, pay off the mortgage, retire, relax and die. Sound familiar?

Although there is nothing necessarily wrong with living this kind of life, is it enough? Not always. Again, because we intrinsically know that there is more on offer than solely going through the motions of this kind of conventional human existence.

Thankfully, there are no upper limits on love and no predestined quota for the quantities of peace that you can experience, for example. So irrespective of where you may think you are today – low, medium or high levels of love, peace or happiness – there is always more waiting to be experienced, but where?

Here exists the common dilemma. Most of us don't know where to find true fulfilment. We believe the inner sense of something missing will be solved once we've fixed, changed, improved or perfected our external world – to the point that it finally fits our ideas of what a fulfilling life should look like.

In this pursuit of "more," it is all too common for us to put our foot on life's accelerator. We end up working and living at ever-increasing speeds, in an innocent attempt to get more done and achieve bigger and better success.

But if we aren't careful, we can end up moving so fast, from one "fix of fulfilment" to the next that we miss the inner presence of peace – that is always present – and the external life that is happening, in all of its glory, all around us.

In 200% Arjuna eloquently explains why we aren't living up to our fully fulfilled potential. He shares how most of our focus, most of the time, is predominantly moving outwards onto our external-life: Get the promotion, meet the perfect partner etc. Rarely do we stop and become still, direct our attention inwards, and in doing so, explore and experience our infinite "inner-world." As a result, with the majority of our attention outwards, Arjuna so rightly points out that we inadvertently end up living only *half a life*.

I can relate this common misdirection of focus that causes so many of us to miss out on living fully. Everything in my life was going great. I had a beautiful girlfriend; we were living in an upmarket part of Edinburgh and driving fancy cars. Career wise, I was working around the world, I had fully-booked *everything*, the money was flowing in and I was even appearing internationally on television.

I was living what many would deem a successful life. The only problem was I didn't feel successful. Something was still missing. I was stressed to the hilt, secretly suffered from anxiety, frequently felt frustrated, constantly discontented and felt a million miles from being the peaceful happy person that I wanted to be.

It was around that time a friend suggested I tried meditation. With the recognition that no amount of external success had brought me inner serenity, I agreed to give it a go. Soon after starting a daily meditation practice, using the same type of meditation that Arjuna is also a teacher of, I found that I started to experience a surprisingly amount of excitement for life, peace and fulfilment.

Not because my external world had necessarily changed or improved, but because I had finally embarked upon the ultimate adventure – the journey within. I discovered that inner peace was possible for me, without my outer performance being negatively impacted. Quite the opposite: I found that inner stillness paid dividends in my productivity within the movement of external life. I now have no doubt that the secret to outer life success is inner stillness.

In 200% Arjuna shares *The Eight Choices for Living Fully*, which are fantastic for cultivating the right rock solid inner foundation for the most fulfilling, and even thrilling, external existence. I invite you to not just read them, but do your best to apply and live them in daily life. I promise, if you do, then you will discover that living 200% is a path of greatness.

One of the standout chapters of this book, for me, is the one on *The Best Ways to Enjoy a Bad Life*. Yes, you read that right – *a bad life!* Not only did I find it to be an amusing twist on the average book of this type, but I also loved how Arjuna so clearly shines a light on the many unhelpful habits that we've all done, at some point, which create both unhappiness and a half-lived-life.

Take life very, very seriously, forget what is truly important to you and *blame everyone else* are the first three of over fifty habits that he so helpfully highlights to us. I believe any life would improve for the better, simply by stopping these first three. Imagine what would happen if you were free from the fifty others too!

When we take life too seriously, our joy speedily slips away. When we make other stuff more important than our happiness or love, for example, then we are on the fast track to frustrations. And when we blame others, we give our power away, suppress our success and postpone our peace.

But if we are willing to take on board a lighter outlook on life, make inner peace more important than our life always going to *our* plan, and quit the blame game, we quickly witness improvements across the spectrum of our life. Living 200% therefore is a superbly simple win-win strategy for a super successful life.

200% is a marvellous instruction manual for anyone wanting more from life. It is a book that holds within it so much real life relatable wisdom. I know this book will change lives because it makes living the best of lives possible for anyone with an inner desire and calling for more.

If *"more"* is calling you, then Arjuna's book is the answer.

Sandy C. Newbigging

Author of seven best-selling books including *Mind Detox*

Welcome to the 200% Club

"It is not death that a man should fear,
but he should fear never beginning to live."

- Marcus Aurelius, Roman emperor and philosopher

By picking up this book you have embarked on the greatest adventure life has to offer: joining the 200% Club.

Members of this unique club have one common desire, one common priority; being truly alive and experiencing life to its fullest – at 200%.

Two hundred percent? Mathematically impossible perhaps but not experientially. Let me explain.

200% of life is the experience of everything.

It is the whole of life: 100% inner connection and stability and 100% outer enjoyment, effectiveness and fulfilment. It is having both inner depth and "soul" *and* outer achievement and adventure. It is having peace *and* performance. It is perfect balance.

You can't fully have one without the other – there is a reason why there are two full halves in the yin-yang circle symbol. Balance is everything.

Success without contentment and joy is half a life. Being "Zen" without action is only half the picture.

It's not an either/or thing. You *can* have both; you deserve both.

You deserve to live 200% of life.

One Important Thing You Need To Know

A life without any kind of stress, struggle, confusion, reaction, self-sabotage, doubt, worry, anger or fear is *completely* possible – yes, even for you.

Just because the overwhelming majority of people experience these kinds of limitations every single day of their lives doesn't mean they are a *necessary* part of the human condition.

Is it possible you don't have to live with any suffering or unhappiness or uncertainty or frustration or any feeling of being lost or wondering what this life is all about?

Yes. You can be permanently free from all of that. *You can.*

I only know this because I've been there. In fact, from time to time my life was *filled* with these things.

For a long while, I would wake most mornings and the fear would be building already, like an ominous alarm I couldn't switch off in my head, sending nervous electricity through my body and tension into my gut.

I found my ways of coping, but I didn't want to simply *cope* for the rest of my life. I wanted the answer; I wanted freedom from these things that weighed me down.

What was worse was I had the feeling that the solution was right there, frustratingly just out of reach.

I was right. The solution *is* so close, you just need to know where to look.

Living free from overwhelm, negativity and limitation and being the very best version of yourself by stepping into 200% of life is incredibly simple and straightforward – when you know how.

You can learn to be constantly clear, calm and content, fully alive, filled with purpose, focused, relaxed, happy.

Life can be profound *and* productive; in fact, it's necessary to have both to get the most from life.

Living 200% is a skill you can acquire, it is a skill you can master. In fact, it's not really something you gain but something you remember – which makes it all the easier.

Like anything, it requires the right knowledge together with a modicum of persistence and a smidgeon of dedication to apply that knowledge. But, really, you need give so little to gain so much.

There are so many misconceptions about living life like this. Most people don't know how simple it can be.

You don't have to become a monk, a nun, a hippy or a recluse. You don't have to give up a single thing – except suffering and stress and limitation. To get it, you just have to learn to look in the right place.

If you have the passion for the fullest, best life possible – or even if you simply want a little more from life – then you are in the right place.

You can have it all – a full and rich sense of inner peace and purpose as well as complete enjoyment and effectiveness in the world – no matter what kind of life you live. 200% of life can be yours.

This book is applicable to all aspects of *your* life, to your whole life. Do these few things that I detail here, and everything benefits.

I've tried to make this message as simple, practical and applicable as possible, so you have the best chance of actually doing it.

You deserve simple. As the artist and scientist Leonardo da Vinci reportedly said:

> *"Simplicity is the ultimate in sophistication."*

In **Part One – How Life Works (and Doesn't Work)**, we'll get to know the two games that make up 200% of life, detail why you would want to master them, and explore what may be currently preventing you from doing so.

In **Part Two – The Eight Choices for Fully Living**, I'll walk you through exactly how to make it so that you can truly live fully.

Let's get started.

How Life Works (and Doesn't Work)

CHAPTER ONE

The Two Games of Life

"A tennis player first confronts the Inner Game when he discovers that there is an opponent inside his head more formidable than the one across the net."

- Tim Gallwey, "godfather" of coaching

In living 200% of life there are two interconnected games we play – the inner and the outer.

The outer game involves meeting the challenges of living but is also about getting where you want to go and doing what you enjoy – your career, work and finances, romance and family, health and fitness, hobbies and sports, possessions, travel and holidays.

In essence, the outer game is what you do to make your way in the world; doing what you need to do to survive and find stability, but also to enjoy, to thrive, to achieve your purpose. It is about performance.

The inner game, on the other hand, provides the foundation that determines the outer game.

The inner game is played against such internal mental and emotional forces as negativity, self-doubt, confusion, fear, overwhelm, regret, guilt, anger and arrogance. The rewards for playing a good inner game are fulfilment, satisfaction, calmness, confidence, direction, focus, contentment, meaning, happiness, peace.

Mastering the inner game makes mastering the outer game simple and straightforward. It takes all the struggle and strain and stress out of living and achieving.

As such, the inner game is primary – changing the inner game affects the outer game directly. The thoughts and feelings you follow direct your words and actions. What you do and say, as well as what you don't do or don't say, gives you your results.

The results of your life are therefore directly related to your internal world.

Mastering the inner game means you can get what you want from life. It involves replacing old limiting patterns and habits and programmes of thinking and feeling, so you don't:

> get in your own way

> stop yourself doing what you want to do

> fall victim to doubt, overwhelm, negativity, anxiety, worry, frustration and anger

> react in ways you later regret

> spend your whole life stuck overthinking the past or the future.

And so you can:

> ➤ focus on this moment in time, on the very thing that is in front of you

> ➤ feel that life has meaning and purpose and direction; that it has a point

> ➤ really enjoy this and each and every moment, no matter what it contains, fully alive, content and satisfied with the fruits of your labours, excited about more

> ➤ live a life of 200% and be a source of inspiration for your loved ones to do the same.

Living a life of 200% begins within – between your own ears – and that is what this book is all about.

The Inner Game – Your Mind, Awareness and Peace

On one level, playing the inner game is about the ability to focus on the thoughts that help you and ignore the thoughts that hinder, limit, distract or cause overwhelm and negativity. It is about making the choices that enhance rather than detract from life.

It is also about dealing with the sheer volume of thought that goes on within our skull – conscious and unconscious thinking is rife, and a real cause of misery and exhaustion.

But mastery of the inner game goes further – it involves the ability to be present and attend to the exact need of the moment, as opposed to holding tight to a plan or an idea of what "should" be happening right now. It is the skill of letting go of a dead past and an uncertain future and living in the same place as your body. Here, now, in this moment: this is life.

At its essence, the inner game is about a particular kind of awareness.

The more this awareness grows within you, the more you come to a rare way of relating to yourself and the world.

Properly directed, your awareness can become permanently conscious of its source; the part of you beyond thought, feeling, and your body. You realise you have thoughts, but they are not you; you have feelings, but they are not you; you have a body, but it isn't you.

Just a moment of this experience alone is a wonderful source of relief and ease.

The growth in this awareness is about remembering who you really are, beyond all the beliefs about who you think you are. It is freeing yourself from the idea that you are limited in any way.

From this experience there is real freedom and ultimate peace – in the middle of a busy and constantly changing world, in the middle of a busy and constantly changing life, in the middle of a busy and constantly changing head, there You are. This awareness is an oasis of permanence and stability; the source of all focus, fluidity, contentment, calmness, happiness, fulfilment and meaning.

Living life from this place is something else. That feeling of supreme "rightness" – the contentment, immersion in the moment and complete flow with what you are doing is superb. A small taste of this can be enough to change lives, forever.

If you understand this, great. If you don't, no problem. Just keep an open mind and read on and you will.

The trouble is, our culture holds several deeply held misconceptions about the nature of mastering this inner game and having these supreme experiences of life.

We talk about stress management as if stress was an inevitability. Very few know how to live *completely free* of limitation and stress without giving up their goals, very few know that it is even possible to have 200% of life.

Fortunately, just because it's rarely done, doesn't make it untrue.

A Common Misconception – Peace *or* Performance?

To simplify, let's take peace as the inevitable conclusion of mastery of the inner game, and performance for the outer game.

Many people ask: "But how can I be full of peace and still get what I want from life?" as if they are two distinct things.

They aren't two different things. Being at peace isn't giving up – and moving forward in life doesn't need to involve stress and struggle. Peace and performance actually nurture each other. You can't live a complete life without both.

So many people sell themselves short, either chasing their goals at the expense of their peace (and health) or chasing their peace at the loss of their goals.

It needn't be this way.

All the great people of this world have both. As business consultant Jim Collins points out in his study of great leaders and organisations, *Good to*

Great, they embody a seeming paradox of having an intense one-pointed focus and will, and at the same time possessing huge amounts of "soft-skills" such as humility and selflessness.

Truly great leaders have direction, boldness, absolute certainty and zero compromise. Yet they also know they are part of a whole and are wide open to more: open to learn; open to change; open to helping everyone rise up. There is no paradox here for them; they know that calmness and clarity is the cornerstone for living the life they were born to live.

These are two branches coming from the same tree: the ability to be at peace and content, and the ability to dedicate your attention to whatever you wish to achieve.

This skill means you *can* access a complete dedication to your goals, a one-pointed focus on what you are called to do, not letting anything stand in your way, *and* have an absolute ability to "let go" and "go with the flow," to be completely calm and present in this moment.

It's crucial that you know that peace and performance isn't an either/or option.

You can have your cake and eat it too. You can. In fact, to live a completely satisfied and fulfilled life you *need* to. What's more, the source of that kind of life is already within you – you just need to know where to look.

Priorities: Performance *Then* Peace?

> *"We treat rest as a reward for hard work. It's not.*
> *Rest and recovery is a prerequisite for being outstanding."*

- Paul Mort, life and business coach

The result of this split between peace and performance is that the world puts doing before resting. Goals, then peace. It's a twisted competitive badge of honour that being frantically busy is seen as a good thing. "How are you?" you ask someone; "Oh busy, super busy," they reply – signifying they're important and they think they're getting things done.

Yet – the overwhelming imbalance on doing is the hugest cause of stress, overwhelm, dissatisfaction and burnout. I would say it's also the cause of so many of the mental health problems our society is saturated with. We've forgotten how to do nothing, how to rest and recharge, how to fully switch off.

Our children? They watch us carefully and learn that exhaustion and anxiety and stress – physical, mental, emotional and spiritual collapse – is the way to live life.

I gave a talk in a class of 10-year-olds recently. "Who gets worried?" I asked them, and the whole class put up their hands. "How often do you worry?" I said, and most of the class said every single day. They're 10 years old and already stressed. A recent newspaper article reported that various suicide help phone lines in the UK were getting on average 60 calls *a week* from kids.

The fact is our culture has it all messed up, totally back to front.

Living 200% of life involves protecting your peace first and foremost. You need peace, calm and clarity because it gives you the physical, mental and emotional freshness, perspective and energy that you need to achieve your goals. Peace and rest are the baseline to any performance.

Without them you're running on empty, like a phone that's about to run out of battery. When you do finally close down? Like your phone, it takes much, much longer to get back into action; when you crash, you really crash – it's a disaster.

"Sometimes the most urgent and vital thing
you can possibly do is take a complete rest."

- Ashleigh Brilliant, epigrammatist and artist[1]

It's so much smarter to recharge regularly, to keep topping up, then you can really get going – and keep going forever.

Without that priority for rest and recharge, there's no clarity, no creativity. You are held captive to the negativity of your head, to doubt and fear, to stress and overwhelm. Exhaustion becomes normal to you – you don't even realise how knackered you are. You're unable to be content either: without the perspective of peace as your foundation, no matter what you achieve, it seems empty.

If you're interested in not only achieving in this world but totally enjoying your time, having great health and being a great parent, partner, friend, boss, colleague, then protecting your peace and your energy is crucial.

Giving Up the World and Becoming "Spiritual"

When I started looking for information about mastering stress and limitation, and about getting into a state of Flow and oneness, I thought the obvious place to look was the spiritual sector. I read a lot of books. I went to a lot of talks given by Buddhists, Taoists, Yogis, Sufis, Stoics, Mystical Christians, meditators, people channeling aliens, you name it.

---

[1] See www.ashleighbrilliant.com for more of his great work

They all *seemed* to talk a lot about renunciation and desirelessness and how that would get me control of my mind and make me happy – and so, being keen and a good student, I tried to give up stuff and live without desires.

I also tried to mimic the correct demeanour, the correct way of talking, the correct way of living and being – but it was all so ridiculous. I was copying someone who was probably copying someone who in turn was probably copying someone else's idea of what was right and correct and "spiritual."

That's the trouble with beginning anything – you don't know when someone's talking rubbish or when you're misinterpreting them. Without qualified guidance, you can wander very far down the wrong path.

Let me assure you – the 200% club is not about renunciation.

You do not have to give up the world, you do not need to give up your desires, you do not have to become a certain way – no matter what some spiritual "experts" on the inner game will tell you, no matter how many people believe it to be so, it's not true.

You don't. Coming to terms with, and loving, who you are and what you love to do is a crucial part of living 200% of life.

Before I knew this, I tried very hard to change myself at a fundamental level.

I tried being a vegan, because that's what I read was the right and proper thing to do. Even though I thought about food all day, even though I got pale and skinny, it didn't matter – it was the right thing to do! I didn't drink alcohol, nor partake in coffee and tea, nor sugar, nor onion and garlic because someone told me they inflamed the passions, and my passions were very much aflame, the pesky critters.

I woke very early to do my yoga, because that's what men of peace did, early in the morning.

I also sat meditating with my legs crossed with a rigid spine for an hour, an air of superiority on my face because even though my knees and back and shoulders hurt like hell, I was stronger than the pain, and could accept it all with equanimity just like the man in the book and on the videos said.

And I felt very, very proud, because I was tough enough to do all these right things, and surely one day I would make it. I would master my mind and get super peaceful. I would enter Shangri-La, or Heaven, or become a Buddha or Enlightened.

Actually, I wasn't too sure what would happen, but I hoped the meaning of life would come along soon because all this hard work was getting to me; I knew when it did, it was going to be good, and worth the struggle.

I tried so hard to be without my desires. I really did. I tried so hard to replace my normal desires with the "spiritually correct desires" and, well, I failed.

And no wonder – without desire you don't even get out of bed. What floats your particular boat is vital to life; it is what gives it sparkle. Without it I found life grey, and a bit pointless. Taking on someone else's desires is completely missing the point, no matter how much its argued they are the "right" way to live.

I look back now and I'm so glad I failed to be someone else.

I remember giving up in relief when, finally, I met a Bright Path Ishaya monk who told me to relax a little bit, to lighten up, to listen to my heart and not do what was "right" but to enjoy what I wanted to enjoy.

All in moderation of course – but a cup of coffee or a steak or a glass of wine could be, for me, very enjoyable things, and I need not scorn them on the basis of an idea. In no way were they the work of the Devil.

I started to see clearly that all my desires could be wonderful things, and that they were a part of me. No one could tell me how to best live my own unique way of life.

I was open to advice, but the best advice that I'd ever received was to look within and learn what was inside my own heart. If I wanted to live a full life, a life of 200%, it was necessary not to deny who I was but accept and honour the fullness of Me, my personality, my desires and my life.

Make sense? I hope so. Don't do what I did, it's not necessary – it's miserable in fact.

The only trouble with desire comes when you hold tight to it, when you insist that your happiness depends on a certain desire being fulfilled in a certain way.

Or you become addicted to a desire. That is when an unconscious pattern of thought informs you that "I can only be happy when I have this one thing that I am addicted to" – when you lose the ability to be present or find satisfaction anywhere else.

Whatever: the thing is, desire is never the deal; it's attachment that kicks you.

We're going to talk about that more later on – but it's always your mental patterns that cause you trouble. It's never about the things, but how you define them.

Peace *and* Performance = 200%

Peace alone is not enough.

Your skills in the inner game are made resilient – mastery is made permanent – through real life, by being in action. Avoiding life, avoiding action? That's not a life, that's not true peace.

Like I was saying, 200% of life involves the embracing of all of your life, as it is. It isn't about rejecting any part of it, nor does it require substantial change in any way.

Sure, you make some small changes – choices that help rather than hinder you; choices that I'm going to detail later on in this book. Indeed, every now and then small periods spent on retreat away from "normal" life are invaluable too.

But the point of any kind of retreat or change is the discovery of deeper depths and fresh perspectives within yourself. What is then essential is the integration of that depth and freshness into the hustle and bustle of your life, exactly as it is.

What is the point of peace and focus if you only have it when you hide away?

What good to you is clarity and contentment if it is lost at the slightest bump?

You want it to be continuous, perpetual – without end.

Recently I returned from three months working at the Bright Path Ishaya meditation retreat in the mountains of Spain. The whole place has a real sense of peace and serenity and aliveness.

But you know what? That is here at home too.

While waiting for a lift to the airport, I picked up some random autobiography of a guy who went to live beside a river in India to find his peace.

He returns to the West after decades of spiritual study and practice and instantly freaks out. The noise, the mass of people, the traffic, the consumerism, the drunkenness, the desire, all the stuff of life.

He completely loses it: he becomes a gibbering wreck until he manages to stumble upon a meditation centre – to him, an oasis of sacredness in the midst of a city of the profane.

How sad.

He's completely missed the point of all his practice. All those years, and he's created a mood, an idea that peace and clarity is only available when the world looks a certain way. "When I'm by my river, then there is peace. When I'm on my mountain retreat, then there is peace."

Do you realise that you, in your own way, do that too?

Simple is Good ... But What if You Can Have It All?

I don't know how many conversations I've had with people who long for a simple life.

Simple is good. But their answer to stress and overwhelm is to chuck it all in and run away to an island in the Pacific. Or they've had enough of Facebook, or their mobile phone, or whatever, and so they're going to delete all their social media accounts and burn their phones.

They believe: "I will be happy and at peace when I get rid of these things."

The fact is, without the right tools they'll wind up bored out of their minds and find ways to get stressed, even in Fiji.

You take your head and your limited and negative patterns with you, wherever you go.

Wouldn't it be easier to simply adjust the way you live life?

Membership of the 200% club isn't about running and hiding. It's about taking action. I know sometimes the best answer is to quit. When you're overwhelmed and can't cope, a perfectly good strategy is to find something you *can* cope with. Sometimes it's about doing different things.

But the fact remains, many times it's about doing the same things differently. Stress is found in our relationship to things, not the things themselves. Stress isn't inherent in the city or in Facebook; it's in how we react or respond to this stuff.

You can find peace and have a really busy, active life. It's important that you don't make them distinct. Because the bottom line is that peace and internal stability isn't about the stuff of life.

> *"Peace. It does not mean to be in a place where there is no noise, trouble or hard work. It means to be in the midst of those things and still be calm in your heart."*
>
> - Anon

Life is here, continually knocking at your door. You cannot avoid it forever. You cannot make it look the way you want it to all the time.

Playing the inner game means peace can be had anywhere, no matter what is happening, no matter where you are – if you know how to tap into it.

All this time you've been looking for peace, it has been within you – and it will be, forever more. Peace is not an experience. Peace is who you really are. All this time you've been looking for peace? You've been it.

Life transforms when you realise this. The circumstances of life don't give you peace, you bring peace to life, regardless of the circumstances.

Permanent peace, freedom and happiness is an inside job.

It may take practise to realise this, but it is the only reality in town.

The good news is, to find peace and joy, you don't need to give anything up.

It's actually kind of funny to think that a path to peace, calm, contentment and clarity requires you to do anything. That you need to try really hard and apply excessive effort. That you might need to adopt a diet or particular hairstyle. That you need to believe anything.

You don't need to change at all, except ... actually ... you will, in all likelihood, make some changes in your life.

But change comes because you are motivated to do it. Not because you "should" but because you want to, or realise you need to; that a bigger, more expansive life sometimes involves doing something different.

What does that "something different" look like? Well, the next chapter explains what it *doesn't* look like.

CHAPTER TWO

The Best Ways to Enjoy a Bad Life

"Everything has been figured out, except how to live."

- Jean-Paul Sartre, French philosopher

Sometimes we are our own worst enemies. Sometimes we're not even aware that it's our own choices which are giving us a "bad" life: a life where stress, unhappiness, anger, anxiety, guilt, regret, dissatisfaction and frustration all arrive unwanted and can be difficult to get rid of.

What are these choices that result in living a less than totally optimal and enjoyable life?

Just to make sure you're clear, below is a checklist of many of the best ways you can enjoy a bad life.

(Warning! I'm trying to be funny, but I'm aware I've been *very* sarcastic. You'll need to be able to laugh at yourself. If you can't do that, you might as well put this book down now and go elsewhere. The 200% club isn't for you.)

Realise that many of these choices are unconscious. You're not fully aware you're making them. But recognising that any of these "best ways you can enjoy a bad life" sometimes occur in your life is a wonderful start. If you're aware, then – and only then – you can start to choose to do life differently.

Don't worry if you recognise a lot – most of us do. I got many of these from personal experience.

1. Take life very, very seriously

Remember – no one gets out of here alive. Life is serious; it's literally about life and death. Whatever you do, make sure you never ever laugh. Especially at yourself.

2. Forget what is truly important to you

Because, as my mum used to say, tomorrow never comes, and leaving the most important things to last means you just never get to them. How wonderful! You can get to the end of your life and realise you never gave any time to what was truly important to you. You also get a big dose of "death-bed regret" – which sounds like a great way to check out of life, badly.

3. Blame everyone else

"It's her fault …" "If he hadn't …"

Philosopher Jean-Paul Sartre once said: "Hell is other people." Even if you have the sunniest of personalities, doubtless you will come across someone at some point who does you wrong or grates on you – and herein lies a powerful secret: if you'd like to guarantee that you live in continuous hell, then blame everyone else for what's wrong in your life. Never take responsibility for anything.

4. Bottle it up, don't talk

When someone does something that adversely affects you, do you:

a) get angry and in a loud voice tell them and everyone around you how much of an idiot they are, and spend the next three days stewing over "That moron"... ?

b) express immediately in a calm, clear manner what you would like them to do, but without holding any expectations that they might listen to you?

c) think you might have misheard them, perhaps they aren't being this way deliberately, maybe it was you who did something wrong, and it doesn't matter anyway, "I'll just let it go" ... then spend the next three days rehearsing the conversation in your head about the way you wished it had gone, regretting not having said what you wanted to say ...?

Which one are you?

Let me tell you something for free – people who can pull off b) are very rare. Stewing in option a) is like blaming someone else (see number three above), and the only result of option c) is that resentment builds then explodes spectacularly, taking heads off (and yours with it). Not pretty.

5. Talk about your problems ALL the time

Because all everyone else wants to hear about is your problems and your story – all the time.

Complaining feels great to your ego and will give you a short-term boost for sure, but as a long-term strategy? An excellent way to make sure your friends are continuously "washing their hair" when you suggest you meet up.

6. Surround yourself with whiney, negative, miserable people

Because that's the only choice you have left after your friends have gotten tired of your constant whining and ditched you.

7. Focus on what is wrong, what is missing or lacking

Try to do this as much as possible. It's the source of good complaining material and means you will totally miss all that is right and good. Spending any time at all acknowledging what is good is *not* a great way to live a bad life.

8. Ignore what's wrong

Sticking your head in the sand in the hope it will go away is a lovely means of exfoliating all those dead skin cells and making sure your life is a disaster – or, at very least, permanently on hold.

9. Insist that this shouldn't be happening to you

An active form of avoidance means you can involve others, if you're smart about it, by getting furious and/or complaining all the time. (Nice try, but it *is* happening to you. Given that, what are you going to do about it?)

10. Wait to be given it, or wait for permission

If you have a dream, just keep dreaming. Do nothing, someone might feel sorry for you and bring it along and drop it at your feet. Maybe.

11. Insist that you deserve it and should be given it

Who knows? It's possible that you might be given it. (Or maybe you'll be given a slap.)

12. Don't ask for help

Trying to handle things on your own is a wonderful recipe for a bad life. You may be shy, or maybe you pride yourself in being tough and independent, but not asking for help guarantees you won't get any.

Everyone should be able to read your mind after all – for a rotten life just wait until they learn to. Never clearly and calmly express what you would like them to do. Bottle it up and wait for the explosion.

13. Never ask any questions

Because then they'll know you're stupid. Much better to *be* stupid than appear stupid – that's a great motto to live a bad life by.

Speaking as a teacher and being involved in helping people – we *hate* questions. It puts us on the spot and requires us to know something beyond what we've been told. And we're not here to help people grow, we just want to get through the pre-written PowerPoint presentation and collect the pay cheque.

(Reminder: yes, I'm joking.)

14. Constantly change paths

Never stick with anything long enough to really understand it, or you may have to truly open up and sacrifice something or discover something about yourself. Then life might have a chance at being better. Not the way to stay with a bad life.

15. Be very harsh with yourself

If necessary, buy yourself a bigger whip and see if that helps.

16. Hold grudges

An excellent way to occupy your time, energy and attention. An extremely useful and productive means to a bad life. And everyone loves a stomach ulcer!

17. Maintain ridiculous expectations of yourself (and others too)

Make sure you are always pushed to the max, are always under pressure, and never feel good enough. Do this and you'll also never be satisfied with what you have already achieved. Excellent!

18. Constantly compare yourself

This is a tricky one – be careful not to inadvertently inspire yourself with comparison, as in "Well, if she can do it, so can I." Make sure you always come up short in your comparisons, because, as Thomas Jefferson once said, "Comparison is the thief of joy," and joy has no place in a bad life.

19. Sleep less and eat more sugar

20. Use the word "should" as much as possible

As in "I *should* eat less sugar." "Could" and "would" should also be used as often as possible.

21. Live in the past and/or the future

Because life isn't really happening right now, under your nose. It's more important to take care of some other time first.

22. Want to be right more than to be happy

Focusing on being right is an excellent way to prioritise winning arguments and scoring those vital "points." People will love and respect you for this ability, and it will mean you never have to understand another's point of view. If you can put someone down at the same time? Wonderful. All in all, an excellent contributor to a small, narrow, miserable life.

23. Never make a mistake or be wrong (or if you do, never admit it)

Whoever said you can't learn without making mistakes clearly had no pride and self-respect.

24. Consider stress a useful tool in getting things done

Stress is, of course, not excitement but overload and overwhelm, and causes not only your effectiveness but your enjoyment to go down the plug hole. Brilliant for miserably spinning around in circles, fast.

Achieving less and making great leaps forward to a heart attack rather than staying calm and clear, free of overwhelm and physical distress? Perfect!

This also has the side effect of making you (at the very least) grouchy and "snappy" all the time. Your loved ones? Keep it up and they won't be for long.

25. Be as dramatic as possible

People want and need more drama in their lives – after all, look at how popular TV, movies and all those books are – they are crammed full of drama. You should supply it too; people will love you for it. Be as dramatic as possible, fly off the handle, make everything a disaster, and all about you.

26. Worry about what you can't control

Consider worry a workout for your brain. Burn mental calories! Get rid of "mind flab!" A great strategy for making sure your brain doesn't get lazy in those quiet moments of your day – such as 2am in the morning.

27. Take on other people's worries too

Everyone, especially your kids, need a role model to help them see the real benefits of worry. Why be content with your own worries? Take on theirs too and they'll grow up knowing how important it is.

28. Never do anything about the stuff you can control

Stay comfortable. Avoid anything that requires anything else. All those amazing things that have happened to you in your past? They all took a leap of faith into something unknown. That took courage, and courage is definitely uncomfortable. You don't want that. Comfort is key to enjoying a bad life, one filled with regret and should have.

29. Stay firmly in control

Never let go, never let up, not for a second. The whole world will fall apart if you do. The tension created within you by single-handedly attempting to ensure the survival of human civilisation will also ensure you're about as fun as herpes.

30. Be a perfectionist

Don't do anything unless you can do it perfectly. Don't let your project be seen until you know it's "just so." After all, you are your own worst critic and your mind will never be satisfied, so listen to those thoughts and ensure that you'll never actually finish anything.

31. Be sloppy

What's the point anyway? Let some other sucker redo it or use it as you left it. Imagine their joy at discovering how little effort you put into it and how little you care about them.

32. Fight, resist, struggle

Never accept what is. Always steadfastly hold on to your idea of what should happen. Seeing clearly, being fluid and flexible, accepting, allowing and adapting? It's for losers. Never stop fighting, even when you have that heart attack.

33. React

Snap, get angry, be impatient; as much as possible. People love it when you're shouting at them.

34. Gossip

Social media has made it so much easier to enjoy a bad life. Hurrah! Gossip is a great conversation starter and time filler. Slagging somebody off – especially on the basis of what someone else has told you – is a guaranteed way of enhancing your social standing among like-minded people. Just watch your back."

35. Feel guilty for doing stuff that recharges you

Why exercise or close your eyes to meditate or read a book or have a tea break when you could be scrubbing the floor again?

Taking time out to recharge your battery by doing the things you love? It means you'll be in a happier, less grumpy mood, less likely to be judging yourself for "Doing it all wrong, again," and then people will miss out on you being a source of misery to them. All in all, *highly* counterproductive to everyone enjoying a bad life.

36. Make it all about you

Make sure that in every interaction and situation, you ask yourself "What can I get from this?" If you can find nothing, walk away. When your life is about helping other people in even a small way? Studies have shown time and time again that your emotional wellbeing, health and levels of life satisfaction all drastically improve, and you don't want that, now do you? Keep life sad, small, dramatic – make it all about you.

37. Give so much you resent them for it

Ensure you never clearly and calmly explain your expectations, or act in a consistent manner with people. Don't communicate at all about how much you feel you're doing around the place because "They should just know." If somehow you're forced into actually talking about it? Never be prepared to see their side of things, or compromise in any way, shape or form.

38. Pine for a long lost nostalgic you

Long gone are the days of the holidays where you planned nothing, jumped on the back of a scooter on some Greek island and camped on the beach; or you had a sleep in; or you partied all night and into the day – because now you have a family or a job or some other form of Responsibilities.

There's no reason you can't keep the glory alive by constantly referring back to that past version of you and resenting what you have now.

In the face of all evidence in the present moment, pretend nothing has changed, your life hasn't evolved and bask in nostalgia. Hold tight! A bad life hates the now, and all the choices you made to bring yourself here.

Long for freedom and happiness that will only exist when life is different, like it was.

39. Over-think things as much as possible

Second-guess, try to predict, over-think. Great for staying up very late at night, for imagining what someone else is thinking about you, for trying to control every possible outcome.

A bad life has an over-active mind at its centre. Think wildly and dramatically and as judgmentally as possible.

40. Forget to speak your gratitude and appreciation

Because they don't need to hear it. Actually saying it makes you feel good too – and in terms of living a bad life, that is a definite no-no.

41. Judge, be prejudiced

Actively judge and be prejudiced about the whole world. You know exactly who and what these people are and what they'll do if you take your eye off them.

42. No second chances

Never give anyone a second chance either, especially if they come and apologise and try to put things right with you. They're definitely up to something.

43. Never apologise

Because you can't do anything wrong. They're wrong – all of them. They don't matter anyway. And saying sorry is a sign of weakness.

44. Be dependent on another's approval

Emotionally chain yourself to other people. Be like a performing monkey and do whatever is required in order to gain their approval. Subvert any part of you that the world might find unacceptable.

A great twist on this is to focus on the one person who doesn't like you. They represent what everyone really thinks of you. Keep this in mind.

Oh – and if a loved one is sad/depressed/in a mood? It's your job to get them out of it; it's selfish of you to be content/happy/at peace if they continue to choose to be caught up in it all.

45. Misery loves company

Help others stay miserable by being miserable yourself – it's really a brilliant way to make sure you enjoy maximum misery in life. Hang out with miserable people. Commiserate, listen to them whine over and over again, but be careful never ever to suggest how they might do anything differently. After all – it's *all* someone else's fault.

Indulge instead, if you think your companion is up for it, in a little competitive misery along the lines of, "Ooh, you think you have it bad, I've got it worse. Listen to this tale of woe ..."

46. Stay on the rollercoaster of life

Make sure your mood and your inner equilibrium are linked to external events. So life is good? Well done – now you can be happy. Life isn't working the way you want it to? Freak out and lose it!

47. Don't bother to stop and smell the roses along the way

You're in a hurry, you've got things to do and people to see, so out-source menial, unproductive life-enhancing tasks: pay someone else to smell the roses for you.

By the time you finally get to where you're going, your sense of smell will have deteriorated anyway.

48. Fill your life with regret

A very handy emotion is regret. Measures of self-punishment, woe-is-me, "should have done better," living in the past, and good old over-thinking all combine to create something sensational. Regret stops you moving forward, from learning from your mistakes, from doing anything really. It's a crucial tool for anyone interested in creating a bad life.

49. Exhaust yourself

Rest when you're dead. It's important to never or rarely recharge your batteries. Exhaustion is wonderful – the more exhausted you are the more overwhelmed you'll be, the more likely depression will descend, the more you can be triggered and react, you won't think straight, and your sense of humour will vanish. #teamnosleep forever!

50. Spend more time at the office

Spending as much time as possible at work is essential because your corporate/government employer will look after you, you just need to dig in a little bit more, for a little bit longer.

Self-employed? Terrific – no one's going to do it for you, and your family will understand why you're never home, and asleep when you are.

51. Be lazy

Never be on time, do nothing when you do turn up, head home early. They're all suckers.

52. Spend all your life thinking about it

Gather knowledge but never actually get going on it. Believe but never put it to the test. Don't get your hands dirty – never head out and experience it. Wish for more but never do anything. Put it off until later. Talk about what you're going to do, for sure, but for a bad life, attempting to actually live it is a waste of time compared with knowing all about it.

53. Ignore that small voice

Whatever you do, don't listen to that small voice that whispers, *"Is this it?"*

Is there a hole in your life that you have no idea how to even begin to close? Ignore that feeling too, for a really bad life has no meaning, and you probably won't find it if you look. Stay on the safe side.

Attempt to black out that small voice that tempts you to find substance to your life, whispering *"There must be more to life than this ..."* by sedating yourself as much as possible. Buy more stuff, work harder, get more drink and drugs in you, indulge in gambling, affairs, porn, gaming, endless TV box sets, trashy magazines and novels, more holidays, more Facebook, more Twitter, more Instagram.

Distract yourself from this voice and your increasing dissatisfaction with life at all costs; otherwise you may find a way out and never enjoy a bad life ever again.

And that would be a shame, and so selfish too – how can others really enjoy a bad life when someone like yourself chooses to leave them alone in their misery?

There You Have It

Fifty-three different and foolproof ways to enjoy a bad life. I am sure there are more, many more, but I didn't want to bludgeon you more than I have already.

Please: don't use this list as evidence that you've gotten it wrong, again. Please: remember to laugh, see the funny side of all this.

Sometimes the truth hurts a little. But the truth is only hurting that part of you that is invested in you living a bad life. It likes being small; it's comfortable and seems secure there.

Shining a light on this part of you is like shining a light on a cockroach; it tries to escape and be unseen as quick as possible. Being unseen means it can continue as it has always done, unchanged – while being seen is a recipe for disaster. Clarity is the first step to change.

The sole reason for this list is so you can see how you get in your own way.

Humans have been doing this stuff over and over again for thousands of years – being unconscious and unaware of what you're doing and how it affects you is not your "fault."

In a sense, it's the momentum of history; you are re-doing what your parents and their parents and their parents have always done, what they consciously or unconsciously taught you to do.

No deal. Don't get into a blame game – but wake up and start to do something different; for yourself, for your kids, for their kids. This is what the 200% club is all about.

Now you're aware of these ways that you are enjoying a bad life? *Do something*. Use them as a springboard to live a bigger, brighter, easier, more joyful experience of life, one where you *consciously choose* to do things differently.

Learning to do things better is something you *can* do – honestly, take it from me.

How wonderful would life be if you did do things better, even slightly better than yesterday? How much easier and smoother would life be? How much more fulfilling?

How much happier would you be, knowing that, with practise, you can make a different choice?

CHAPTER THREE

Your Life is Your Choice

"There is ultimately only one lesson to be learned in the practice of life ...
***I choose**. I choose how I feel. I choose what I do. I choose what I want*
and what I don't want. I choose, over and over and over again, moment
to moment, breath to breath. And the culmination of those hundreds
*of thousands of millions and trillions of choices equals **my life**.*
Which I am responsible for because I am all grown up.
Because I am an adult."

- Kim Christie, photographer

Life is made up of your choices.

Life isn't about what happens to you – life is how you decide to respond to what happens. Life is not about the *what*; it is all about the *how*.

The circumstances of life are one thing. How you choose to react to these circumstances is everything.

There are so many self-help books on how to change the circumstances of your life. This is not one of them, not really. This is about how you can change the one thing you are *fully* in control of: your reactions and responses to life – the inner game.

This one small thing – your ability to choose – is the key to everything.

Developing free choice to rise above the chaos gives you the experience of 200% and being the very best version of yourself.

Choice is the foundation of Life with a capital "L." Without it, there is no ability to effectively do the things you want to do; there is no simple calm or contentment; there is no effortless focus.

Everything in life transforms when you gain this ability to choose.

Are you content muddling through this existence or do you really want to have the best life possible: a life of 200%?

If it was truly down to just a simple choice, what would you choose?

Peace or Pain?

As an outdoor instructor living in a beautiful house on the edge of a lake in a small, thriving mountain town in New Zealand, I thought I had set my life up perfectly – I had everything on my wish list.

I had incredible, funny, inspiring friends, several flexible jobs that paid well and yet gave me plenty of free time to do the things that I loved to do. I had money, proximity to some great rivers and mountains, and the time and the energy to exploit all of the above.

Slowly but surely however I came to a place where nothing made sense.

I thought initially I was depressed, and perhaps I was; certainly it was a very frustrating and confusing time. Everything pointed to the fact that I should be overwhelmingly happy, and yet I wasn't. Outside success, in terms of "all boxes ticked," did not add up to inside contentment.

That little voice that whispers to so many, *"Is this it? Is this all that life is about?"* wasn't whispering to me anymore. It was shouting.

I thought I was living the dream. I thought I had taken a step sideways, ignoring the obvious rat race traps I felt I saw so many wrapped up in; I thought I had life sorted, and yet that inner voice, again and again:

"You're wasting your life."

Why the voice, so insistent? Why was I so confused? Why was I feeling so unhappy? Why couldn't I just stop thinking so much? Why couldn't I be content with what I had?

I found myself in a downward spiral of sorts. I became more aware of how incredibly harsh I could be to myself, and how judgmental I could be of others; a perfectionist who wished others would at least try to sort themselves out as well. I couldn't hold a relationship down because of this, and well ... I didn't know what I wanted.

I even broke down in tears driving home one afternoon. For no reason, I had to pull over as I took a couple of minutes to cry myself out.

Why?

God knows; I didn't.

I wasn't a total mess – it's not like suicide was on the horizon. I was confused but coping, and yet however good life looked like from the outside there was definitely something big missing, and I had no idea what it was.

I began looking for more – in even more kayaking adventures, in yoga, alternative therapies, silent retreats, in psychedelic drugs and even in conversations with mediums who channelled beings from outer space. I was pretty open to trying anything to find an answer to that nagging voice and get some lasting peace of mind.

Eventually, I learnt a meditation technique called the Bright Path Ishayas' Ascension, and it really clicked with me. Now life started to have meaning – and quickly too.

A few years after first meeting my Bright Path Ishaya teacher, Maharishi Krishnananda – a very funny, warm and sometimes intense American man, an ex-Vietnam war veteran and some-time presidential advisor to Ronald Reagan (not your typical "guru") – he told me that his greatest wish for all his students is that they see how they, *and they alone*, create peace or pain in their lives.

These words make more and more sense every day.

This book is an attempt to clearly convey this choice to you. This choice that you have to create heaven or hell for yourself in each and every moment, regardless of the circumstances you find yourself living in.

Once you see how you are constantly creating peace or pain for yourself? A permanent choice for peace is indeed possible.

Asleep at the Wheel

With this understanding I now see how in every step of my life I have always had the choice to move towards peace or move towards pain ... *always*.

Yet at the time I had no awareness of what I was doing. The choice for pain was largely unconscious, it was habitual.

I didn't know I was choosing for pain, and you don't either – after all, no one wants to be in pain, no one wants to be in misery and confusion and anger and worry – and *if* I was aware of it, I had no way of stopping, of choosing not to.

It's the same with everyone; we're largely asleep at the wheel of our own lives. Doing our best, but just not really aware of what we're doing to bring ourselves peace or pain.

The Answer

Regardless of how it happens, the answer, the bottom line is always:

What you put your attention on, grows.

In both significance, momentum and in "weight," what you put your attention on, grows.

This happens for anyone. You and your life are no different, as much as you'd like to think you are.

When you focus on what is wrong, what is missing, what is painful or dissatisfying in life, you create a movement, a momentum of thought towards that.

Continue placing your attention on what is wrong or lacking – *even* with the intention of doing something about it – and you create a downward spiral; one that gets faster and deeper and more confusing and miserable the more you feed it.

The longer you stay focused on the things that bring you pain, the harder it is to remove yourself from it. You create a monster, one that sucks you in and has such momentum it seems like your free choice and enjoyment of life goes with it.

For many people the only way out at this point is distraction, even tranquillising themselves. To temporarily ignore the monster in your own head through the use of alcohol, drugs, TV, Facebook, reading, the internet, gambling, shopping, junk food, overseas holidays ... anything to find a little relief.

Right?

The Stressed Survival Brain and the Downward Spiral

In an attempt to keep you safe and happy, a significant part of your brain exists to point out danger to you: in other words what is wrong, what is missing, what is dissatisfying. A very handy thing indeed. Until it's not.

Of course, the basis of learning or growing or doing anything different is realising that something is not working or needs to change. Obviously, this is a very useful survival and growth mechanism. You wouldn't want to be without it, sticking your head into the sand and pretending everything is fine when it's not.

The trouble is that this part of our attention is activated *all* the time for most people.

When I talk about creating your own monster by what you focus on, I'm not talking about simply noticing unpleasant things you could take action to avoid, or things you want to have or could do better at ... I'm talking about the *continued* and *ongoing* (and largely unconscious) focus on what is wrong.

Many people lead fast, demanding, stressful lifestyles. This means the survival-based fight, flight or freeze response – that all humans possess – gets turned on all the time.

You know it – it's the almost automatic response to a threat meaning you get ready to fight something, or run away as fast as you can (flight) or stop and play small (freeze) so perhaps the threat will not see you or will ignore you.

Definitely useful when there is real danger ... but it gets switched on constantly. For example, when in traffic you start to white knuckle it and yell at people; when your streamed movie gets stuck halfway and won't restart and you want to throw the computer across the room; when you're in that high powered meeting and instead of saying what you really think, you play it safe and choose to follow the crowd by nodding your head; when your kids or partner do something and you choose to give in to the irritation and "red mist" which means you snap and are yelling at them before you even really notice; when you stand up in front of a group of people and you lose all clear thought, turning into a gibbering wreck; when you're queuing and the moron in front of you is paying in pennies.

Now, the more you operate in this fight/flight/freeze mode, the stronger that brain centre concerned with threat and survival becomes.

The stronger it gets, the more hyper-alert your attention becomes, the more it tries to watch out for, predict and manage the next threat. The more you focus on what's wrong, the busier and more anxious and angry your brain becomes.

The more you focus on what is wrong, the more you're moving towards a life of pain.

If you've ever lain awake at night with your brain whirring about all the things you have to do, and what went wrong today, or what could go wrong tomorrow, you know exactly what I'm talking about.

Can you perhaps see how one small choice, constantly made – even unconsciously – has a huge effect in terms of your overall choices in life?

Can you see how an inner choice to focus on what is right and good, or on what is wrong and missing, affects your attitude to life? Which in turn affects what you do and say, which gives you the results of your life?

Can you see how you choose for peace or pain?

CHAPTER FOUR

The Big Benefits of Choosing Big

"Oh, I don't really think about that, because it's wasted energy, isn't it? What's done is done, we can't change that, but we can change the way we cope with it."

- Diane Piper, when asked her feelings on the men
who raped and threw acid in the face of her daughter Katie[2]

The Wisdom of Choosing Your Response to Life

Everyone has challenges. Everyone has troubles. Everyone has problems in their life.

But what amazes and inspires me is seeing people who have lived or are living through horrific things and yet who shine, full of gratitude and love for their life as it is.

You might call them "glass half full" people.

Then there are those with comparatively event-free lives who grumble and complain through every little inconvenience: "glass half empty" people.

---

[2] Katie Piper was attacked by an ex-boyfriend and an accomplice. She now heads a charity for people with burns and scars, as well as being a TV presenter/personality.

Why is that?

As we've talked about in the last chapter: you constantly choose your response to life.

This choice defines how you live, regardless of the circumstances you find yourself in. I'd like to repeat that last bit: *regardless of the circumstances you find yourself in*. You are not different from anyone else – no matter how much you think you are. This applies to you too.

Your choice is total: you decide whether you live in peace or in suffering. No one and nothing can cause you to suffer: you choose to suffer.

I know it doesn't feel like this. As I was saying, no one wants to suffer; everyone is looking for a way to avoid it. The trouble is we don't know how. Furthermore, suffering has become normal; it's almost expected as "part of life."

Being constantly happy is viewed with suspicion by some. If you decide not to suffer it's almost like you're not being "real" – whatever that is.

I had a friend who fully realised her choice to be totally at peace with the world. One day, she was taken aside by an acquaintance in the street and asked if she was on drugs.

Bizarre isn't it? Happy lady, walking down the street, therefore she must be taking drugs.

Those, like Buddha and Jesus, who have transcended suffering are elevated to a mythical status, beyond humanity: they must be Gods.

Yet the truth is:

> *It is your human birthright NOT to suffer.*

True! Your birthright is to have absolute sovereignty over your responses to life.

From this basis, complete freedom from suffering is a given. It *can* become your normal way of living, your natural response to life.

In doing this, you will:

- end overwhelm and stress – "I've got too much to do and no time to do it; It's not happening the way I want it to"

- no longer feed negativity – "I'm useless; I can't do this; I'll never get it right"

- unchain your happiness from external events and others' approval or good humour – "It never goes right for me; They don't like me; I need them to be happy"

- ditch anxiety, worry, regret and guilt and over-thinking – "I did it wrong; I am doing it wrong; What will happen? I need to be in control"

- stop being scared about making mistakes – "I'm terrified of it going wrong; What if I mess up?" – and become bold and adventurous

- stop reacting unconsciously – "Oops, I did it again" – and start being able to consciously choose your responses to life

- no longer live in the past and future – "Life was/will be so much better" – so that you can enjoy this moment as it is and who you are, as you are

- fill that hole, that feeling of "is this all there is?" – and find satisfaction, purpose and meaning.

Far-fetched?

Not at all. I've seen this transformation in myself, and in countless other members of the 200% club. If it's true for one, it must be true for all.

Freedom of Choice

Wouldn't it be cool if you could choose how you felt?

Wouldn't it be awesome if you could just be happy, no matter what?

Wouldn't it be great if, instead of reacting and getting all wound up, you could choose to be all Zen, and just flow through?

Or if you did react to something, if you did get angry or mad or sad, then you could just choose to drop it when you wanted to?

What if you didn't even have to choose to act in the ways you wish you would – that your natural and automatic reaction to life was one of calm, clear, happy, attentive, aware, grateful, compassionate Aliveness?

Wouldn't *that* be cool?

Actually, it *is* cool to live like that.

It's not just a pipe dream, and it's important for you to know it's achievable for you.

It makes life so much easier. Instead of carrying anything, you are able to just let it go and get on with what is in front of you. Instead of being swayed by doubt or worry, instead of controlling and straining to get what you want, you can just effortlessly focus and, with the minimum effort, get the maximum result.

It's much more fun. Being overwhelmed by your emotions or being pulled this way and that by what life brings you, holding grudges and maintaining arguments – now, that isn't much fun, is it? But living with complete free choice and being happy for no reason at all? Very, very fun.

Living a life of constant free choice is possible for you, if you want it. It is also simple. All it takes is practice, the right kind of practice. That is all.

The only reason you hold onto anything is because of a habit. The only reason you react to anything is a habit.

Why not create a new habit?

> *"We are what we repeatedly do.*
> *Excellence, then, is not an act, but a habit."*
>
> - Aristotle, Greek philosopher

This Isn't Difficult, It Isn't Hard

This doesn't require hard work. It does require commitment, but then so does anything worthwhile.

Even something as simple as going shopping requires you to maintain focus for long enough to reach the store and purchase what you want. It's the same with experiencing freedom from being yanked around and pulled to and fro by the habitual programmes of your mind and emotions.

Forming this new habit is as simple as this:

1. Know that the way you experience life is your choice

2. Exercise your choice

3. Keep doing this until it becomes second nature, until you have freedom of choice.

I realise all of this is simple to say. I get that. I get that there is a vast difference between simple to say and easy to do.

I know: I've been there, I've whined about it. But if I can get better and even good at this, you can. I will never suggest you do anything I haven't tested myself. This is not theory – it has to be practical.

Here's the thing – I will show you how to form this new habit, and then you begin.

I suggest you practise when life is easy, when the going is good. Then when you need it most, you won't need to work at it. It'll become as simple as I say it is. You'll become like human teflon, stuff that used to stick and create havoc will just slide right off, and you'll be laughing all the way to experiencing the best possible life.

If you want it, and do what is necessary, you'll become it. There is no other option. You can't fail. As Buddha reportedly once said:

"There are only two mistakes one can make along the road to truth; not going all the way, and not starting."

The question then becomes: "How? What do I do? Which direction do I go in?"

CHAPTER FIVE

What Do You Want, Really?

A Fundamental Understanding

First things first – we need to come to an understanding. We need to talk about what is the most important thing to you.

Because if you know what is most important, and where to find that, you are up and running towards living a life of 200%. You will have taken a huge step forward in being able to freely and consciously make your own choices.

What Is the Most Important Thing to You?

> *"If you don't know what you want,*
> *you end up with a lot you don't."*
>
> - Chuck Palahniuk, author

If you have ever met a Bright Path Ishaya such as myself, chances are they would have asked you a question:

What is the most important thing to you?

To say it differently in three similar ways:

If you could have one wish, and one wish only, what would that be?

If you could give your loved ones one thing, anything at all,
what would you give them?

At the end of your life, when you look back,
what will you wish your life to be filled with?

Everyone I ask this question gives the same answers.

They want to be content, to be at peace, to feel love, to be free. They want to avoid suffering, hardship, misery, sorrow, dissatisfaction, stress.

For simplicity, I will say that all of these things are some version of peace or happiness – they're all on the scale of the ever-changing possibilities of "good" that humans can experience.

Even if you want freedom from misery, let's agree to say that itself is a form of peace, or of happiness. Then it's clear that when it comes down to it, peace and happiness are the most important things to everyone. Everyone just wants to be happy.

Interesting huh?

The most important thing to all of humanity isn't material. Everyone on this planet – even though they may think otherwise – doesn't *truly* want financial security or perfect health or a soul mate.

These things are very important, I agree, but they are actually second tier. They're not *the* most important thing to you, and I can prove it.

Answer this question for yourself before reading on:

What would financial security or full health or an amazing relationship bring you? How would you feel if you had these things?

That's right: a feeling of no worries, of being content, loved, happy, free, at peace.

So, what you think is most important to you might not be *the* most important – actually, peace and happiness is.

Please realise that I'm not saying health and financial security and relationships aren't important; that you can or should toss it all away and sit under a tree. That's been tried before.

What I'm saying is that it's important to realise what you're *really* trying to get from life, otherwise you end up chasing the wrong thing and wondering why it doesn't really satisfy.

It would also help if you realised that you can be content and at peace without perfect health and perfect financial freedom and a perfect relationship – and it's crucial that you are. These things take time to build or to get. But you can be perfectly happy right now, if you know how.

Peace and happiness, the most important thing to you, is the best foundation for your life. From it, everything you build on top comes easier with more clarity, with less stress and struggle, and every step along the way becomes more enjoyable and fulfilling.

Without a solid foundation, all the material possessions and experiences in the world won't satisfy.

You may achieve and get and do great things – but there will still be a hollow feeling, a sense of something missing, a sense of lack of meaning or purpose.

You may temporarily distract and divert all you like with more achievement and/or with drinking or partying or shopping or Facebook or gossip or sports or gaming or burying yourself in books or music or *whatever*, but that nagging sense of pointlessness will always resurface.

So: find your foundation first. Prioritise it. Be Happy.

How To Find True Happiness and Peace

How many people do you know who are happy all the time? How many people are constantly living life to the fullest?

Not many, I imagine, based on what I've seen on the news, the internet, and the people who I have met, watched, bumped into, walked past and sat next to throughout my life.

Why doesn't happiness come naturally?

Well, it does, actually.

It is your true nature to be happy.

Seriously, you weren't born with stress and negativity and doubt and drama. As a baby, if you weren't hungry, sick, and didn't have a full nappy, it's very likely you were pretty darn happy – naturally and without effort.

Grab a baby – they are alert and joyful. After being upset they quickly return to a smile, they don't hold onto the past. They know how to play, to explore, there's no limitations, no sense of "I can't, I'm no good." There's a total innocence that is wonderful to witness. They have nothing to prove, they have nothing to hide, there's no concern with presenting the right image to someone else.

You were like that too – yet, slowly but surely, you forgot.

You picked up beliefs and judgments about yourself and the world around you. You burdened yourself with responsibilities, stresses, struggles, dramas. You forgot the quiet joy of being alive and became your obligations and plans, you became your stories, you got serious.

Peace and happiness stopped being a simple, natural thing – it started being dependent on certain things and certain people. It became externalised and conditional, something that had to be achieved and gained. Your beliefs became less and less flexible, you stopped being so explorative and open-minded, you started cementing "I can" and "I can't". You became more and more regretful of past events, more worried about future ones.

However, just as you acquired all these things, it's possible to leave them behind. It's possible to ditch all your mental constructs and limitations. It's possible to break all the chains and the walls that you unwittingly set up around yourself.

It's possible, and actually very simple, to be continually happy and at peace and to never suffer again, even *with* all your adult responsibilities and challenges – if you know how.

All the wise sages, philosophers and teachers of the world, from all cultures throughout history have said the exact same thing. Happiness and peace *is* your true nature.

There *are* people in the world today that experience this. They live complete lives of 200% – full and rich, joyful and content, all while taking care of their responsibilities and creating and achieving, and without a scrap of stress, struggle or drama in doing so. Although they may not be many, they show it is possible for anyone. They show it is possible for you.

Honestly:

What if? What if life does not need to be full of ups and downs? What if it didn't have to be full of struggle, exhaustion and drama?

These things are not inevitable; they don't have to be part of the deal. Suffering is not necessary, I promise you.

If you don't believe me, that's okay. If you just like the idea, then you are in the right place. Just assuming it is a possibility is the first step to experiencing complete happiness and contentment in every aspect of your life.

So, the question really is:

*Why aren't you completely happy **all** the time?*

CHAPTER SIX

Why the Problem Isn't the Problem

The reason happiness escapes so many of us is because what we think is the problem isn't actually the problem at all.

The fundamental problem of all humanity is that we don't see clearly what causes happiness to come, and we don't see what causes happiness to go.

We get it all wrong.

Looking for Happiness in the Wrong Place and the Wrong Time

Indeed, most people don't know where to find happiness. Do you? If people knew, they'd have it all the time, no matter what they're experiencing in their lives.

We have it backwards. People think:

*"**When** I get x, y and/or z, **then** I will be happy ..."*

For example, you might think that you'll be truly happy when you get a new partner or that new job or more money or that shiny new car or when your health improves or you hit that target. Or you may think you can only be happy when you're doing this or that or the other thing, when you get away for the weekend, when you're seeing your favourite band or out on the town or having an adventure, when you're doing that thing you love.

Nope. Be happy first. Don't make your happiness solely dependent on getting or achieving or doing something. Because if you do, not only will it be externally caused – meaning it's out of your direct control and choice – but you'll also be waiting for it. Your happiness will always be in some other moment.

Unchain Your Happiness

Stop looking externally for an inner experience. Stop looking for something to *bring* you happiness or someone to *make* you happy and find it within.

Happiness and peace is an inside job, always and forever. Things don't make you happy – you decide to be happy. Happiness is never given to you; happiness is an attitude that you choose, no matter your circumstances:

It is never the situation.
*Only, always and forever it is your **reaction** to the situation.*

Happiness is not just caused, it isn't just a reaction to nice events. It is chosen.

*It isn't **what** you do; it's **how** you do it.*

Remember? It isn't *what happens* to you; it's how you *react* or *respond* to what happens to you.

You aren't so much in control of the external circumstances. You'll probably *try* to be in control, but the fact is your ability to control the world around you is always going to be limited. What you are totally 100% in control of is your responses.

If you are looking to get happiness from a person, in money, in possessions, in your health, in a job, in travel, in anything – you are setting yourself up to miss out, always.

Don't get me wrong – the good things of life are to be enjoyed and appreciated. It's also wonderful and even important to celebrate achieving goals and milestones.

However. Unchain your happiness from being *solely* caused by these things – otherwise you'll always be dependent on them for happiness.

The problem isn't just that you can't be happy because you don't have the things that make you happy. The problem is more that your happiness is dependent, conditional on certain events or things or people happening, and that is the opposite of freedom.

Don't Look for It Later

When you believe that your happiness is externally caused, it'll pretty much *always* be some other time in the future:

*"I'll be happy **when** ..."*

Because you're relying on something to give you happiness, it's always coming later ... with the weekend, or the pay raise, or the dress size, or finishing your project, or doing your favourite thing.

Do you see that? You're waiting for happiness. When happiness is dependent on something external happening, you constantly postpone your own happiness for a future moment.

That way of seeing happiness means the chances are you rarely have it now. At the very least you don't have it nearly as often as you *could*. You might hope it's coming in some other moment when this or that happens, but where is the ability to freely choose or secure happiness for yourself as you are, where you are, right now?

The most important thing to you becomes like a carrot you dangle at the end of a stick – so often just out of reach. You're running for happiness, but it always seems to shift. Like a mirage, you think you're getting closer and closer, only to find it appears to be over the next hill.

This hunt for future happiness causes you more stress, strife and unhappiness than you realise.

You think, "When I get home I'll be happy." You hit a traffic jam and your happiness is all of a sudden a way off, and how infuriating is that? "When my baby stops waking in the night, I'll be happy." Your baby wakes constantly and so your happiness gets further and further away. "When I get away kayaking, that will make me happy." You sit, staring out the window dreaming of your favourite thing, resenting the office job and the fact the weekend won't happen for days (that was me, by the way).

Don't delay your happiness and peace. Don't postpone it for *when*. Choose to have it now. Let happiness come with events and things – enjoy them – but don't let your most important thing live in the future. You may never get there.

Even if You Do Have It, It Soon Slips Away

So, you have the thing you think will make you happy, and it does! It's wonderful, what fun, how alive you feel ... but it never lasts. It soon slips away, doesn't it?

My friend bought a brand new Tesla he'd been longing for. A beautiful machine. But the glory of it lasted mere days, the happiness that it brought him soon forgotten, undermined by fresh concerns.

The human mind has an amazing propensity for throwing away the happiness of today in anticipation of the happiness (or troubles) of tomorrow.

It's aptly said that the mind is like a monkey jumping around, branch to branch, searching for the perfect banana. It finds one but throws it away as soon as it sees another "better" one.

You have the thing you want ... and then your mind discounts it, it becomes ordinary, you take it for granted and so you chase the next thing.

Or, because you think your happiness is caused by something, you become hyper-aware of what will take it away from you. In this state, you rarely enjoy the moment because your mind quickly gets busy trying to predict what will remove it.

"Bring on the weekend" you think, "that will make me happy." You spend the week living for the weekend but spend a big chunk of it (most of Sunday) dreading the upcoming Monday as your mind sees your happiness ticking to an end. Or in relationships you're needy and clingy with an irrational suspicion of your partner, simply because you're scared they'll run away. What you focus on, grows. Ironically the very things you do to try to protect your happiness can bring about its downfall.

Not being able to choose your own happiness means life will be a constant rollercoaster – which means you have no choice: you're sometimes up, sometimes down; you're always looking for the next up, and fearing the next down. You're never present, never truly living free, never in control of your own happiness and contentment and peace.

Do you now see why happiness can seem so elusive? We've been conditioned to look for it in the wrong place at the wrong time.

What Sylvester Stallone Knows About Happiness

I started to see the happiness problem clearly only after I'd spent some time searching for things I *thought* would make me happy.

Going kayaking seemed to make me happy. But ... it was a certain type of kayaking. When my skills were sharp, when I was performing well – then, and only then, was I happy. When I was performing poorly? I got frustrated and angry.

When my girlfriend was in a good mood? I would be happy. When she wasn't? I spent a lot of energy trying to make her happy. If that failed I'd then get angry and frustrated with her.

You see the pattern?

When you choose to be happy regardless of the circumstances of your life, happiness has a chance of becoming your ongoing experience – it can become a solid base and foundation to all of your life.

If you have this solid, happy foundation, everything you add to it will only be more and more enjoyable and life affirming. If you have no foundation, nothing you throw on top will satisfy.

Make sense?

Sylvester Stallone found the exact same thing. He once told the story of how he thought fame and fortune would bring him happiness. He worked hard, became reasonably successful and found he didn't have the happiness he was looking for. He looked around and saw that his rich and famous friends didn't seem that happy either.

So, he worked harder and became even more rich and famous, and yet still didn't find the happiness he wanted. Again, he looked around and, if anything, he saw more unhappiness among the super rich and famous he'd just joined.

It was then that he woke up to what caused what.

Life does not bring you happiness. You bring happiness to life.

There may be wondrous or terrible things on the horizon, but regardless, you can choose to be happy, right now.

I know it might not seem that way. I'm not talking about a "false" happiness, like some kind of positive affirmation that we actually don't believe. I'm talking about making real peace and happiness the foundation of everything you do, every step to every goal you chase, every moment you live.

How do you do that?

The way you do that is to fully show up for life and be aware of where you're putting your attention. It is the one thing you are in control of, the one thing that cannot be taken away from you.

Look within. Learn to have happiness that is uncaused, learn to choose to enjoy everything. Don't delay your peace and happiness, choose to have it now.

The Real Cause of Stress

Stress (as in excessive pressure and negativity) and happiness don't live together – that much we can agree on. But what causes stress?

Stress is commonly believed to be caused by an event or person we don't like, something that we find unacceptable and overwhelming. Yet stress is just like happiness – it doesn't happen *to* you; it's chosen *by* you.

I know this might be a big pill to swallow – after all, there are definitely things you dislike in life. When they are not in your life, it is so much easier to be happy.

Let's have a closer look though.

Take a moment and write down all the things that cause you stress, that you dislike, that you'd prefer weren't in your life.

Go ahead – make a grand list of things, really go for it.

When you're finished, take a mental and emotional half-step back and look objectively at what you have – as dispassionately and with as little emotion as you can.

Step 1: Stress and Your Reaction

Recognise that your stress list is uniquely personal. Not everyone will have the same list as you. Right?

Now, are there any items on your list that inherently cause stress? In other words, do they cause *everyone* stress *every* time they appear? Because if they did, then you could say that was indeed a cause of stress.

Let's take Christmas as a simple starting example. For some people, it's one of the most stressful times of the year, and yet for many it's one of the most fun times of the year.

So, it's not Christmas itself – there's nothing inherent in it that is stressful. It's something about an individual's reaction to Christmas that creates stress.

How about work: do all people find work stressful all the time? Do you?

No, all people don't, and you don't either. It's an individual's response to particular demands of work at particular times that determines stress.

Okay, let's go for something juicer: death and dying.

Is there anything inherent in death that is stressful?

For sure, some are afraid of, or at least nervous about, dying. I think that's pretty common in the West. But for many cultures dying is seen as a great release, a transformation into a greater state of being than this current existence. Or it is seen as simply part of the cycle of life, like another, slightly more mysterious stage of maturing – such as leaving behind childhood and becoming an adult.

Death is then either celebrated or, at the very least, not a cause for stress.

Do you see what I'm getting at?

There is not one thing on your list that is *inherently* stressful. None of these things cause stress for all people, all the time.

Stress therefore lies in your personal response to the things you don't like. Now, in terms of freeing yourself from stress it's important to see this. The things you don't like *do not* cause you stress; your *reaction* to these things causes you stress.

I'm not saying you have to *like* these things, not at all. I'm saying get clear on what causes you to get wound up about it; the flying off the handle, the overwhelm, the anxiety, the suffering – because then you can do something about it.

No one likes to be stressed. If stress is inherent in any of the items on your list, there's nothing you can do about it. But if stress is about your response and ultimately your choice, then you *can* do something about it; you can start to free yourself from the source of all stress.

How wonderful would that be?

Because when you get stress-free, then you can also choose to be happy, no matter what.

Step 2: Stress and Control

Head back to your list. Of all the things on there, which items can you change immediately? i.e. Which ones are you in control of, now?

You may be able to see how you can make different choices sometime in the future: for example, your job. If you dislike your job, you could choose to get another. However, this can take time and isn't under your immediate control (although people do quit to run free and deal with the consequences later all the time).

Take traffic as another example.

I used to hate being stuck in traffic. It "caused" me so much stress, so I'm an expert on this one.

You can take precautions such as researching any accidents along the route, you can leave at a time of day which avoids obvious delays, such as the school run or everyone going home after work.

But beyond that, when you're stuck in traffic, you're stuck. You can't do anything. You have no control.

What causes you stress is not the traffic – it's your *reaction* to the traffic. Again:

What causes you stress is your focus on what is wrong right now.

All you can see is how late you're going to be, how bored you are with hopping along, speeding up, slowing down, how frustrated that the lane you find yourself in always moves the slowest, how you want to be free to just drive, how you want to be at home with your feet up, how you want to be anywhere, but stuck here.

What do you have control over? You can't control the traffic – but you can control your levels of stress.

You choose stress and pain by focusing on what you don't like. How stressed you get depends on how much focus you bring to the "wrong," to the "shouldn't be."

It's all for a good yet misguided reason: you think that when you get rid of the problem you can be happy again (some time in the future), but what you're actually doing is creating more of a problem and delaying your happiness further.

What You Focus On Grows

Like I said earlier, your awareness is creative. What you choose to notice in your life grows in significance. You can choose to notice what is wrong with your world and your life, or you can choose to see what is good and right.

When you get stressed, what happens is that you have grabbed hold of a notion that what is happening to you is not right. "Something is wrong!"

This is fine. It's good to know what you like and dislike, what you would like to keep and what you would like to change. However, the problem is you *fixate* on what is wrong so much that you can't see anything else.

You can't let it go. It cycles around and around in your head. You can't be present with what is in front of you. This complete grip of "wrongness" means you get stressed and you lose perspective; you lose joy and calmness. What are you doing to yourself?

You Think Happiness Happens When Problems Go

Life is just like a gigantic buffet. There is a huge array of wondrous things to experience.

But say, for example, you don't like beans. What happens when you get stressed is a little like saying, "What! Why are there beans here? Why am I experiencing beans now? It stops me from having everything else that I want. This is ridiculous!" etc, etc. You become so involved in the beans that you forget everything else in your buffet that is good. Stress is never about the beans.

Stress is caused by the habitual focus on what is "wrong" and the attempt to remove it.

Is it possible to have a problem *and* also be calm and stress-free with it? Yes, it is. When you do this, you're much more able to deal with the problem in an efficient and creative manner.

Is it possible to learn how to do this? Yes. Learning how to do that is what the second half of this book is all about.

Before we get there though, it's crucial that you realise happiness isn't removed or stolen by some external problem. You remove yourself from happiness by trying to fix the problem. Stress comes when you think the problem must go before you can be happy again.

Are you starting to see why the way you have been chasing peace and happiness has resulted in stress and suffering as well?

Now, it may also help to understand four common reasons why you're not as happy as you want to be.

Four Common Reasons Why You Aren't That Happy

1. Happiness isn't actually that important to you

The most important thing to everyone is to be happy. Everyone just wants to be happy. We've talked about this. But would you honestly say that happiness and peace is the most important thing to you?

Yes?

Yet you don't prioritise it. You aren't committed to it. It is well down your list of things to do.

Your lists are full of the urgent things to get and to achieve and to do, and then, right at the bottom, last on the list – when you have time – is to be happy.

You want to clear the decks, then be happy. True?

"When I get rid of my problems, when I get my jobs done ... then I can relax, and only then, I can be happy and at peace."

It doesn't work, does it? You never get there. Your happiness is delayed for a future moment; but, most importantly, it isn't a priority. You never give it the attention you say it deserves.

If you are interested in being happy, you have to make it a priority, now.

Make happiness the core of everything you do in every moment – regardless of what's happening in your life. Make it first and middle and last. Train to be happy. Make everything – every action you take, every response you make – about seeking genuine, internal happiness in this moment. Choose, then choose, then choose to be happy. Choose your attitude in all that you experience. Keep it as a priority, forever.

Then, and only then, it comes and gets you.

You realise that you are happy for no reason at all. Nothing can give you happiness; you just are it. Nothing can take it away either. You may prefer things to go a certain way, but either way you are happy.

You have happiness that is uncaused.

Practise your choice to be happy, and not to be stressed. You may need some new tools for this. You will need to prioritise and to practise, but that is all. Prioritise it, make it first, and everything in life gets easier, immediately.

2. You don't believe it's possible

You've settled for less. You don't believe you could be continuously happy for no reason, completely content, at peace. You believe that suffering is part of being human.

That's not true.

3. You don't want happiness badly enough

You won't listen to a word I say if you're not motivated enough.

You don't know why you should do something different from what you're already doing: "Life is pretty good. It has its ups and downs for sure, but it's alright. I'm pretty happy, all things considered."

Well done you.

But you're a victim of the "Curse of a Pretty Good Life," where life is cruisy. Not cruisy as in filled with freedom of choice in a totally stable, solid, smooth, happy and peace-filled way, but cruisy because nothing really bad has happened in your life.

Because nothing bad has happened, you haven't really been tested, you've never found yourself in a hole and therefore you're not really aware of the reality of your own mind. You don't know how chaotic it can get, you're not truly aware of how out of control your reactions can be.

Which is wonderful, lucky you – long may it continue. Perhaps if you do find yourself suffering and realising you don't have as much freedom of choice as you think you do, then these words might come back to you.

But if you have suffered, if you are aware of how nasty, chaotic, reactive and fear-filled your own head can be, in a sense you're blessed. Because now you might be motivated to do something about it. You're motivated to get much, much more from life.

Another thing:

You're probably not prepared to give up what you think you know.

Stress is the known, just like for some people being obese or alcoholic, or whatever limiting pattern they experience, is known. If you stop being stressed, or stop being so frantic, or stop constantly planning and controlling and analysing and judging – what will fill its absence? Who are you without these limitations?

Indeed, who are you?

4. You believe it's selfish to be happy

People really do think it's selfish to be happy. Some people still think the earth is flat too.

I know mums especially can have a real problem with guilt. They will put themselves last, they will delay their own happiness because they care so much about everyone else.

Yet when you're happy, all your loved ones have a better chance of being happy. When you're miserable? Everyone around you knows it; *everyone*.

When you prioritise true happiness and the conscious choosing of your responses to life, you win and they win. You become a solid role model and source of true stability, so they can find freedom and 200% in their lives. How wonderful is that?

It's not selfish to be happy. It's contagious in the best possible way.

Ready to go for it?

PART TWO

The Eight Choices for Living Fully

CHAPTER SEVEN

The Prerequisites for Raising Your Game

What Do You Need To Enjoy Freedom of Choice?

As you start to understand that you choose peace or pain, and are free to choose whatever you like, you'll probably also notice that you have some habits, patterns, and programmes that *seem* automatic. They seem to take you into a negative, downward-spiralling state without you appearing to have any choice at all.

So, even though you would *like* to choose and respond differently, sometimes you just react negatively or in a limited fashion – the result being stress, guilt, blame, fear and victimhood.

These patterns aren't automatic or inevitable. You learned them through your experiences of life, and you can un-learn them too.

Overcoming the momentum of unconscious choice is a simple matter of having the right practice: a practice of re-training your attention to move towards peace and clarity when those seemingly automatic patterns and habits want to take you towards pain and confusion.

Continued long and consistently enough, this practice will form a different automatic habit – one that allows you to naturally and *habitually* choose for happiness, peace and freedom, not limitation.

This is just like heading to the gym to get stronger or leaner, or learning how to play a musical instrument, or how to speak a language, or training for any other new skill. To enjoy 200% of life you just have to take the right steps and keep taking them.

I will give you the right steps – eight choices in all – to take, and an understanding of why you'll want to take them. The understanding is unnecessary. It is useful, but not vital. What *is* necessary is to make and re-make the choices.

The following are excellent principles to keep in mind when you're pursuing your 200% life.

Stick with these and you will get the most out of your practice:

1. Commitment

2. Innocence

3. Take nothing seriously

That is all. Nothing else is required.

1. Commitment

Commitment is the ability to make some small changes and the gentle persistence to keep doing them. It is fundamental to learning, gaining or becoming anything.

In fact, commitment is the single greatest quality that will bring you what you want.

Commitment isn't harsh. It's not about violence. It is about discerning what is important to you and choosing to focus in that direction.

Of course, it involves sacrifice – you can't do everything, so you have to discriminate. Some choices take you towards your goal, some take you away. If you want to get to where you want to go in the shortest amount of time, this necessarily involves a restriction of choices. However, this does not require harshness.

Anything that you have now is because you made a commitment to it: a commitment of heart and soul to dream it, to say, "Yes, this is important to me;" and a commitment of body and mind to follow through in reality, to say, "I won't let anything distract me."

The time you give every day to something is a great indicator of its importance to you. We say so many things are important, and yet so often we shrug our shoulders and say: "I just don't have enough time."

Yet if it was truly, absolutely, crucially, vitally important to you, you would find the time. My fellow Bright Path Ishaya, Priya, puts it beautifully:

> *"'Not having enough time' is not a reason for something you can't do,*
> *only an excuse for something you don't want to do."*

If it's important to you, you will find a way. If not, you'll find an excuse (as Anon once said). Many times, it is just a matter of gaining perspective.

You need perspective because the chances are you, like so many people, confuse the urgent for the important. Dwight Eisenhower, former President of the United States, said:

"I have two kinds of problems, the urgent and the important.
The urgent are not important, and the important are never urgent.
Now this, I think, represents a dilemma of modern man."

Humanity is lost. As Eisenhower said, we're rarely able to "give the important the touch of urgency" it deserves.

That is precisely why our lives are filled with busy-ness and yet feel hollow and unsatisfying. It is why the grass always seems greener on the other side of the fence; contentment is rare.

It is why we have no real stability and we're shaken so badly when life gets tough. It's why there is so much stress and unhappiness; it is a huge part of why the West has so much material wealth and yet our rates of addiction, crime, suicide, depression, anxiety, sleeplessness are through the roof.

When you think about what is truly the most important thing to you in your life, consider: How much time every day do you personally spend making sure it becomes a reality?

You say it is the most important thing to you, but I am willing to bet a large amount of gold bullion that it actually ends up way down on your priority list. You delay it until after you get a bunch of other more "urgent" stuff done; in reality, this means you rarely ever get to it.

And that's a shame, because what is truly important to you gets delayed and postponed, sometimes indefinitely. You end up on your death bed and only then does it all become clear because there's no more time left to postpone it.

Do you want to continue to delay and postpone the most important thing to you?

If you really had perspective on what was important it's likely you would be well on the road to already having it:

"Our outer world reflects our inner commitments. If we want to know what we're really committed to, all we have to do is look at our lives. We are, whether we are aware of it or not, always creating exactly what we are most committed to.

It is vital to understand that the choices we make are always in alignment with our deepest commitments. By examining what we have and what we don't have, we will be able to uncover and see what we are truly committed to."

- Debbie Ford, self-help author

Gain some perspective on what is really important, and commit to that, truly.

Important Everyday Things

"If it's important, do it every day."

- Dan John, throwing and lifting coach, and religious studies academic[3]

You want to create habits to ensure that what is important to you is reflected in each and every day. You really don't want to live any other way. You don't want to get to the end of your life and realise you

---

[3] Brawn *and* Brains, Flesh *and* Spirit: I love it when people confound either/or expectations and pigeon-holing.

procrastinated it away. You don't want to end up in your last days with any regrets – at least this particular one, which you can now avoid.

The great Chinese philosopher Lao Tzu once said that, "A journey of a thousand miles starts with a single step," but a journey of a thousand miles is also completed by many steps in the same direction.

Commitment = Consistency

Make commitment only about the consistent steps that you take every day towards your goal. Make any judgement of short term success or failure irrelevant. Make it all about learning and improving. In the journey of transforming a life you're only going to get better and better.

The fact is, if you have the right attitude, this journey is open ended – you are never going to stop growing, which is an exciting and wonderful thing. Constant growth, never-ending expansion? Huzzah! How wonderful.

But know this: there is no journey without commitment; just a wandering in circles.

Motivation and Inspiration

What's *your* motivation for committing to living a life of 200%?

Your motivation, your "why," is important, crucial even. When you find out why something is important to you, you'll have a huge source of lasting commitment. You'll have a reason to stick at your practice much longer than you will by relying on inspiration alone.

You see, you won't always be excited, you won't always be inspired.

Think about all the New Year's resolutions that fail. Apparently, according to one study, more than 90% don't last – a third fail in the first *week*. That gym membership, those brand new running shoes or DIY project in the back of the cupboard, that "learn a language" app, the guitar sitting there waiting for you to pick it up.

You know very well – excitement and inspiration can leave as quickly as they come.

The human race is full of good intentions. People are full of short-term commitment and motivation and inspiration ... *and* they are also full of failure to keep going on a long-term basis.

Commitment involves doing things that – sometimes – you don't feel like doing, that you're not too excited about. (But take note; this is different from a whole life spent doing things you don't want to do, or doing what you think you "should" do. What a waste.)

True motivation is far removed from just thinking that you *could* or *should* do something different. It's also far removed from just feeling *excited* about doing something different.

The most powerful motivation that fuels the consistent commitment to take you through any ups and downs comes from the realisation that you actually *need* to do something different. If you want a different result, you *have* to change.

You can find your why in two ways.

First, ask yourself what you want more of in your life. Maybe you want more peace, more patience, more freedom, maybe it's something else.

Ask yourself:

What is truly important to me?

What do I really want more of in my life?

How will my life be if I actually have that?

Can you get this by doing everything exactly the same as you are now?

Second, ask yourself what you want less of in your life? Maybe you want less stress, less reacting, less negativity. Will this happen if you keep going exactly as you are?

Ask yourself:

What happens if I don't make any changes?

What happens if I don't do anything?

What happens if I stay the same?

It may be that you get more motivation from avoiding pain than from seeking pleasure. That's okay. It is often said that change only happens when you realise the pain of staying the same is greater than the pain of changing.

Be honest. Seriously – if you continue in the same way, what is the end result?

I once asked someone this question and he said quite simply: "I'll die, and quickly, leaving my wife and kids alone."

Avoiding pain is a powerful reason to commit to something different – and I found precisely that. It was *very* important to me that I never went back into the dark holes I had been in. Avoiding that pain gave me considerable reason to get over the inertia and do something different.

My motivation for making a success of going full-time self-employed as a meditation teacher was so I never had to go back to the office I used to work in. I still remember saying goodbye to everyone. I was walking out the door when I heard one voice: "He'll be back," it said.

That sealed it. My pride now would not allow me to even consider quitting full-time self-employment and going back in there. I had to make a go of it.

You'll be the same. You may want to prove someone wrong. You may not want to let someone down. You'll find there will be quite a few sources for your reasons why – but they have to be important to you. No one else matters, but you and your reasons do.

Be really honest with yourself, do some digging and find out your personal reason why – then you'll have a great source of commitment.

When you find out what you want and why, and having seen that you need to change, don't procrastinate, don't think about it, jump in – do it. Start the commitment. Time is short, and procrastination makes it fly. Do something, one small thing at the very least ... just do *something*.

2. Innocence – A Fresh Attitude Changes Everything

"We do not see things as they are; we see them as we are.
We do not hear things as they are; we hear them as we are."

- The Talmud, Jewish text

The world is created by your expectations. You see what you expect to see. If you wish to engage with the world fully, as it is, you need to drop these filters to reality.

As filters, your mind and beliefs truly alter everything. Every single experience is determined by your thoughts and beliefs that are active at the time.

What is real? What is true? You probably don't even realise it – the process is so unconscious and "normal" to you – but you rarely experience reality. You're actually experiencing your own mind.

This is where it all gets a bit like the movie *The Matrix*.

It's like you live in a box that is defined by your expectations and judgements. When you start dropping these expectations, the walls become thinner, more see-through. You wake up from a mind-created reality to an experience of what is true in your life.

The self-imposed limits to your life also start dropping; a wonderful state of affairs as you wake up and see clearly how you chose pain, how you chose limitation. In this awareness you're able to make a different choice, resulting not only in less fear, stress, anxiety and overwhelm, but way more joy and peace and contentment – all uncaused, all just because. Nothing to prove, nothing to hide.

The world is so much bigger, brighter and easier outside your self-defined box.

The Bright Path Ishayas refer to dropping your expectations as innocence. I like that.

To break it down for you:

Innocence

= having no expectations = no preconceived ideas = no prejudice
= no self-imposed limits or filters = openness
= calm and clarity and contentment

There is no better way of instantly experiencing more peace and joy than being innocent. You want clarity and creativity? Experience this moment without prejudice. Having no preconceived ideas about any person or situation means you can experience things freshly, exactly as they are. Instant freedom.

Furthermore, you only experience suffering in life when your experience of it does not meet your expectations: "But this should not be happening!" The stronger your expectations, the greater the trouble for you. Recognise this?

When you are innocent you also try more things. There isn't a fixed sense of "I can't" or "It won't work for me," you just explore. The world can then open to you in surprising ways.

Innocence also has a sense of play about it. If you're really being innocent and fresh, you cannot possibly be taking anything seriously. Taking things seriously is always the end of both enjoyment and creativity.

By the way, innocence does not mean naivety. It means being open to life changing in unexpected ways. It means having the flexibility to accept this change, thus being in a position to cope, to adapt and react creatively, to enjoy the ride. Innocence is about having no self-inflicted boundaries. It is an easy, fun, peaceful, sane way to live.

Innocence is so important. It is a nice balance to commitment. Without innocence, commitment can get harsh and rigid. Without commitment, innocence can be like wandering this world humming "everything's perfect" without actually going anywhere. They complement each other nicely.

3. Take Nothing Seriously – Non-Attachment

"Have strong opinions but keep them lightly held."

- Philip Goldman, business coach

"Laugh at what you hold sacred, and still hold it sacred."

- Abraham Maslow, psychologist

"Sacred cows make the best hamburgers."

- Mark Twain, author

You may have noticed that the times things get sticky for you are also the times you take things seriously.

Seriousness means constriction. It comes from holding onto something tightly: "This is the way it must be!" It means you cannot be open or flexible or receptive to anything else. You can't be innocent.

Holding tight or being attached means you are guaranteed to hit up against something. Conflict and suffering become inevitable. When you hold tight and take things seriously, it's the spark that invites a fight. You will set yourself up in opposition to others, but also to nature itself.

Nature is change. There is the old story comparing the oak tree with the willow. When a strong wind blows, the oak, standing stiff and unmoving, cracks and breaks; the willow is able to bend with the wind – its strength is in flexibility.

The answer is to be innocent and to not take anything seriously, even that which is most important to you.

Never make any absolutes – the universe loves to prove you wrong. Certainty is a nice thing, but just as important is being open to discovering more. It costs nothing to be receptive and flexible. Then you can be light and not serious, always.

When you have a sense of lightness, it automatically means you have things in perspective. Perspective means you have clarity; it means you aren't getting sucked into a drama. Then you can make the most of what actually *is* happening rather than trying to stick with some plan of what "should be" happening.

Make no demands. Have preferences for sure, but insist not. Hold onto nothing; set nothing in stone.

When you don't play the game, you are removed from it. Job done. There is no struggle, ever. So, don't even invite a fight; just take nothing seriously. Stop playing the game.

Do this and you will find that the difference between you and your opinions becomes clear.

When someone challenges an opinion that you hold tightly, you believe they are challenging who you are. You see this happening so much in the world – taking things personally leads to so much misunderstanding and conflict.

Your opinions are not you. Your beliefs of how things should happen are not you. All beliefs are simply an *idea* of what is true from your point of view at this point in time.

The truth is much closer to you than any belief.

So, keep what is most important to you as a priority. And that isn't about being right; it's about being happy and at peace.

At least I imagine that is true for you. Unless being right is more important to you than your mental, emotional, and physical health and wellbeing, in which case go ahead: insist on being right.

But I'd advise you to take nothing seriously. Have fun. Be aware and learn to laugh at everything, most crucially yourself. A wise man once said that if you can do that, you'll have a source of entertainment forever.

CHAPTER EIGHT

The Fundamental Choices of Life (With a Capital "L")

"Grant me the serenity to accept the things I cannot change,
The courage to change the things I can,
And the wisdom to know the difference."

- The Serenity Prayer of Alcoholics Anonymous

The Zen of Doing and Not Doing

Mastery of Life lies in the mastery of the above three skills: the ability to do nothing, the ability to make change, and the presence and wisdom to realise when to do what.

Doing nothing is just as important as doing. Yet while many of us are excellent do-ers, not many can truly do nothing. That is why it comes first.

Many times in life you cannot change a single thing; you must sit back and accept. There is no other option. Reality is undeniable – except this can take an incredible amount of time to filter through our dense skulls.

Fighting and struggling and insisting against reality is hard work. It's about as effective as trying to push a mountain out of your way. Yet that doesn't stop you trying.

How many times in a single day do you kick against something you cannot change?

For some reason you don't see what is happening – you only see what "*should*" be happening.

As long as you fight and push against "what is" you get stressed – you lose all your cool, all your humour, all serenity, all innocence and appreciation of this moment. You're stuck in your expectations of what should happen – and it stays that way – until you accept, or reality changes.

Acceptance can happen in a heart-beat; sometimes reality *never* changes. Want to wait until everything matches your idea of what it should be?

In acceptance, you are surrendering to what is. You give up your insistence of what should be happening in exchange for peace and perspective: an excellent trade-off.

Acceptance isn't giving up. It doesn't mean you don't care. It's simply stopping a useless and draining fight. Instead you are able to see clearly and work with what you have, within the situation in which you find yourself. Clarity means you can be creative. There lies fluidity and freedom, and great serenity too.

Acceptance is king in all spheres of life. Learn to accept.

The Courage To Change the Things You Can

"The only true failure in life is inaction.
Don't be the person who lets every opportunity pass them by."

- Pat Flynn, fitness coach and philosopher

Life is also about action. If you don't do something, nothing will happen.

What do you want to do? It is your choice. After you decide, you need to follow through.

All of this may require courage.

Now – needing courage to do something is an excellent sign that it is important to you. Keep walking in that direction. Everything that has been important to you has required a jump into the unknown. A gulp and a leap. As tempting as it may be, don't avoid it, do it. Avoidance is never a path of satisfaction.

Have courage, be bold.

The Wisdom To Know the Difference

Lastly, the wisdom to know what to do comes from being very alive to what is being presented to you in this moment. Then, and only then, will you be able to meet the need of this exact moment – the only moment you have where you can actually do anything.

Wisdom comes from experience – from learning from your mistakes – but it also comes from a connection with your inner source of clarity. Some might call this intuition. It is the ability to know what is right; for you, now, for this moment. It's the ability to gauge your inner state, as well as the state of others: when you're resisting and when you should act; when you can keep trying and when you should give up.

This ability gets stronger the more you tune in to this precise moment in time. When you are alive to now, you can indeed meet its exact need.

So, be fully present and alive to now. See what this moment requires and let the next course of action be revealed to you. Wisdom also lies in patience – the ability to wait and see what is needed, what can be done.

When you know, do, or do not – but be wholehearted in your doing, or not doing. Don't sit on the fence.

Okay? Nothing worse than living a life half-arsed.

The Eight Choices

An incredible life – not only for yourself, but everyone around you – stems from these attributes of serenity, courage and wisdom.

Some people spend a lifetime cultivating just one or two of these abilities. How do you ensure all three are not just a lofty aspiration, but a constant, lived experience?

As I see it, eight fundamental choices lay the foundation for a truly great life – one that is paved with serenity, courage and wisdom but also fun, freedom and fulfilment, and more.

The essence of living a life of 200% is being fully focused, calm, and happy; the end of stress and struggle. All that is good about being human lies in mastery of these following choices, in the order we're going to talk about them:

Choice 1:   To Own It (when you want to point the finger)

Choice 2:   To Respond (when you want to react)

Choice 3:   To Accept (when you want to reject)

Choice 4:   To Appreciate (when you want to criticise)

Choice 5:   To Give (when you want to get)

Choice 6:   To Be Here Now (when you want to be somewhere else)

Choice 7:   To Be Bold (when you want to blend in)

Choice 8:   To Be Zero (when everyone is telling you to be someone)

Be assured, these eight choices are simple. They may not be easy – because of past habit – but they are simple to make into a new habit.

CHAPTER NINE

Choice 1: To Own It
(when you want to point the finger)

Take Full Responsibility – the Crucial First Choice

Of all the choices you can make that will transform your life, this is the most important. It is a defining moment in a life: when you decide to grow up and stand on your own two feet.

Membership of the 200% Club can only begin when you decide to take full and complete responsibility for *all* of your life. For all of it! For how you feel, how you react, for what you say and do – but also for what happens, for your results, for everything, for *every single part of your life*.

Taking full responsibility is a bold move, but nothing can really happen without you embracing it.

Wait! Before you jump in:

Do not take this decision lightly.

It means you can never blame anyone else for anything ever again. It's not about them any longer. It's all on you.

Why is this so important?

Making this decision is incredibly freeing. Your life is now up to you; you don't have to wait for anyone else, you don't need permission, it's all *You*. You own this. You're firmly in the driving seat, in control of all your choices.

How exciting, huh?

"But," you may say, "there are obviously things that are not in my control" ... and you would be right. How can you possibly take full responsibility for, say, your results when there are so many seemingly random, impossible-to-predict events that impact things?

"It's Not my Fault" – Pointing the Finger

There are numerous conditions and circumstances that mean being, doing and achieving what you want to do becomes difficult. There are numerous reasons why you can't do something. To many people you'd be extremely justified if you pointed the finger at all these reasons to explain why you can't or didn't or won't.

Clearly, it's not your fault – and you'd be 100% correct: it isn't your fault. This and that and her and him all have an impact on your results in life.

However ...

In living 200% of life we're taking this up a level; you're stepping up from merely whose fault it is. It's not about blame any more.

Making the choice to own every single part of your life, even your results, is all about how you're going to play this game of life, and play you must:

"Nothing surpasses the holiness of those who have learned perfect acceptance of everything that is. In the game of cards called life one plays the hand one is dealt to the best of one's ability. Those who insist on playing not the hand they were given, but the one they insist they should have been dealt – these are life's failures. We are not asked if we will play. That is not an option. Play we must. The option is how."

- Anthony de Mello, Jesuit priest and spiritual teacher

Of course, there's sometimes precious little control in life – as the saying goes, "Shit happens." Often you're dealt things you'd never choose. The croupier of life does deliver external ups and external downs.

But how do you want to play this?

Do you want to spend all your time and energy pointing the finger and blaming some event or some person – and in the meantime, doing nothing at all?

Or ... are you going to take up the challenge of the game and play to your fullest, with the cards you've been given, doing your best to get better cards?

Do you want to continue to react unconsciously, focusing on everything that went wrong?

Or ... are you going to respond with awareness, not making excuses but making deliberate choices based on what you can do now?

Do you see the difference?

Do you see the simple, and yet incredibly powerful beauty in choosing to take full and complete responsibility for *all* of your life?

Such a bold choice, but it means you never spend any time focusing on what went wrong, or what could have been.

Life gets exciting and so simple because you're playing with the cards you have, not the ones you "should" have.

You stop playing in a world of right and wrong, and start playing the real game of Life – not wasting a single second on anything except for "What can I do?" and "What am I going to do?"

The benefit of this choice is that you get full control of your life – ironically in a world where there is precious little control – because no matter what happens, you decide to play from there with what you have.

For want of a better word, it's extremely empowering. The most stress in life occurs when you're taken over by a feeling that you have no control. By assuming full responsibility, you get full control. Not only that – it's the end of stress and overwhelm.

You stop being a victim to circumstance. Instead of the situation defining you, you decide to define the situation – exactly as you wish.

It means the problems that you're faced with now have value to you. Because you take full responsibility for them, the question is no longer about whose fault it is, but really about what you can learn from the situation.

"How did I contribute to this?" is a valuable thing to ask. Pointing the finger and making excuses means you never actually see how you can do things differently and better.

Taking responsibility means life becomes about progress, not playing it safe.

I realise this is easy to say and harder to do. I realise this means you're in the spotlight, and your ego can't shift the blame anymore.

However, if you're wanting to step up and live a life of 200%, you have to stop pointing the finger – no matter how justified you feel. No matter where you are or what happened, you always, always have choice.

"Why Is This Happening to Me?"

One of the clear indicators that you're pointing the finger, that you're falling into the role of being a victim to the situation, is this question that you will ask that (perhaps unknown) deity in the sky:

"Why is this happening TO me?!"

Ever asked that? Of course you haven't. But should you find yourself shaking your fist at the sky at some impersonal, uncaring supreme being, take a step back and take responsibility.

When you take full and complete responsibility for everything that happens to you, then, and only then, can you turn it all around to your advantage:

"Why is this happening FOR me?"

An excellent state of affairs, wouldn't you agree? Perhaps that supreme being that threw you into what seems like a mess actually isn't so uncaring after all?

Your choice when faced with any challenge is either to retreat into victimhood or to embrace it – use it for your greatest good to become more awake, more aware, more conscious, more free.

Owning Your Own Happiness

Critically, taking full responsibility means you're not waiting for someone or something to make you happy.

You're deciding that you will rely on nothing to bring you what is most important to you in life: you take full responsibility for your own happiness.

No longer will you delay your happiness or your peace for a future moment. Instead, you're deciding that you will do what it takes to find happiness and peace right now, whatever your circumstances.

That is it. It doesn't get any more simple than that:

Take responsibility for your own life; then choose happiness and peace first and foremost.

Do this and you will come to a point where you'll realise that to choose anything else is madness. And therein lies true wisdom, and freedom too.

CHAPTER TEN

Choice 2: To Respond
(when you want to react)

In taking full responsibility for your life, you are assuming complete ownership of everything you think, feel, say and do, as well as everything that happens to you – for all your results.

In doing so, you set yourself apart.

It is a declaration of independence. You are declaring your intention to develop complete and conscious freedom of choice – a state of being where your levels of happiness and peace don't depend on anything external.

This is already revolutionary. As we've discussed, everyone believes that what they want – to feel good and not feel bad – comes from someone or something external.

It creates such suffering and stress because they *need* to have certain things happen and to keep happening so that they can feel good.

You're unchaining yourself from this – completely enjoying the fruits of your labours but not depending on them to make you happy. Having happiness that is uncaused means you do stuff because you *want* to, not because you *need* to.

In doing so, you also declare the intention to practise the fortitude, flexibility and presence to ignore any negative and limiting thoughts and feelings. You're declaring independence from the ups and downs of your own mind; instead you're choosing to follow that which contributes to your greatest good, and the greatest good for all around you.

Instead of unconsciously reacting, you're choosing to practise consciously responding.

This involves developing full awareness. Awareness gives you the ability to examine your thoughts and reactions. Without awareness there is no free choice; without awareness there is only blind reaction rather than freely responding.

Awareness brings freedom.

Reactions Are Quick

One of the greatest challenges to awareness and free choice will be those habitual thoughts and feelings that come seemingly quicker than thought – or at least quicker than your ability to choose something different.

Reactions ARE quick – sometimes you get triggered faster than you can choose not to.

Bad news creates rapid panic, anxiety and/or anger before you know it; your partner saying something "stupid" means the fire burns fast and nasty, and spiteful words are out of your mouth before you can even think about what you want to say. You then spend the rest of your day chewing over what you could have or should have said.

But you *can* develop the ability to develop a "half-step back" from events, other people, your thoughts, emotions and reactions, meaning you get more time to counter the reaction and choose how you want to respond.

You *can* root out the causes of these triggered reactions, you *can* re-programme your brain to respond with free choice.

The first step is indeed taking full responsibility for these reactions and responses. No one ever *made* you feel a certain way or do something, you chose to. The other step is creating an environment where you are more able and likely to choose to respond rather than letting a reaction run.

Reactions Can Be Useful

First of all though, reactions are useful indeed; it's wonderful to be quick off the mark. It's wonderful to be able to do things automatically, without thinking.

I'm not saying you want to become slow and ponderous, overthinking everything. Overthinking anything is a recipe for disaster.

The trouble is not so much reacting, it's when the reaction is dictated by negative habit or limited programming. When you more or less automatically do stuff that doesn't serve your greatest good.

Later on, in the 8th choice, I'm going to talk about a way of living that is automatic but that comes from a place of "purity" within you. This involves "clean" conscious responses that do serve your greatest good, totally free of limitation. But until then, I'm sure you know exactly what I mean when I talk about blindly reacting. We live it enough on a day-to-day basis.

Now, unconscious habitual and limited reaction and triggering is one thing, the consequences are another: being consumed by the aftermath, the regret, guilt, and recriminations from reacting in ways you're not proud of.

You snap at your kids and then you regret it, because they didn't deserve the scale of your reaction. You stay regretful and self-violent for the rest of the day.

Your colleague at work directs a throw-away comment at you and at first you're shocked, then appalled, and then angry and frustrated – at them, but equally at yourself because why didn't you stand up for yourself and say something?

A kid at your child's school dies of meningitis, and the anxiety amps up, you're left thinking and thinking of how you might explain to your child about disease and dying and how they might react.

You know? There's the reaction, and there's all the time wasted spent thinking about what you've done or not done.

A great many people don't have lasting peace and happiness because of their reactive triggers. They constantly get discouraged and quit because of them. They are, seriously, like a monkey on a chain because of their reactive triggers. They get pulled to and fro all over the place by them.

If you want different results in your life, if you want freedom from drama, guilt, anger, worry, overwhelm, negativity, of being consumed by past words or actions, not able to let go, then you'll want to respond in ways that serve you, not hinder you.

How do you do that? How do you get that "half-step back," the clarity to see your options and choose? How do you reinforce quality, clean responses, habits and programmes?

First, let's understand the processes at work.

The Brain Chemistry Behind Your Reactions

An external event causes two reactions – a chemical reaction in the body and a thinking reaction in the mind.

The event is one thing. You can't control this (though you can try – people try and cotton wool themselves from life all the time, and yet this level of control never seems to give them the security they desire. I digress – we'll cover this in a future chapter).

Correspondingly in the body there is also a rush of chemicals and hormones. Left to their own devices, as neuroscientist Jill Bolte Taylor explains in her book *My Stroke of Insight*, these chemicals can be gone, completely flushed through the body, within 90 seconds.

You can actually see and feel this happening in yourself – you'll need to get super curious and aware and watch yourself closely. There is the trigger event and then a flush of activity in the body. You feel "something" surging.

Notice how your mind will then label it: "I'm angry," "I'm panicking," "I'm getting upset" etc …

If you follow the label, the mind will create a story. It draws on all your past experiences with similar events, it tells you whether you like the feeling or whether it is a cause for alarm, and exactly what you should do about it: fight or run or freeze, make yourself small.

But if you ignore the label and story and just watch; like a wave building to a peak, the feeling crashes and withdraws – the chemical reaction is over quickly, in less than 90 seconds.

If you don't offer this process any resistance you can witness it all coming and then going – building, crashing, leaving. It's over; done with.

I see this happening in my six-month-old daughter all the time. Something loud or shocking happens, or perhaps she rolls over and smacks herself on the head.

She reacts for sure – she jumps or screws her eyes up at the bright lights shining in her eyes; she cries in pain.

But the reaction is done and over with super quick. She's back to smiling in no time – all because she has no labelling process, no stories, no judgements, no resistance ... yet. The event is just an event, intense perhaps, but it doesn't mean anything.

Adults, however, definitely do have judgements and stories.

When you're unconscious to it, your mind kicks in, labelling and judging and resisting and planning and overthinking. The result of all this mental processing means beyond the initial reaction the feelings are stimulated all over – and over – again.

After the initial 90 seconds, as the neuroscientist Jill Bolte Taylor puts it so well:

> *"Any remaining emotional response is just the person choosing to stay in that emotional loop ... if you continue to feel fear, anger, and so on, you need to look at the thoughts that you're thinking that are re-stimulating the circuitry that is resulting in you having this physiological response over and over again."*

The event is one thing, the body's reaction is another, but the ongoing reaction and over-thinking? That's your thing. That's where you can create choice. It is where the saying "pain is inevitable but suffering is optional" begins to come true in your life. Choosing to stay unconscious to your reactions is you choosing for suffering over peace.

Reactions are habitual, hence you need to practise choosing for a conscious response. The more conscious and aware you can be, the more "space" you'll have between the event, the body's chemistry and your mind's labelling and ongoing circular thinking and emotions about the event.

The half-step back begins right here.

Exhaustion – the Spanner in the Works

I thought I was pretty aware of my reactions. I've made it one of my life's dedications to be aware and see how my mind gets triggered – and then, in this awareness, choose for something else. Yet in becoming a new parent, another factor has been introduced, one that affects so many people: exhaustion.

We were in the labour ward, tired after three long days and nights (baby did not want to come out) but happy with a successful, straight-forward birth. Everyone's quiet, relaxed, at peace.

The cleaner comes in and drops her metal bucket on the floor at the foot of our bed – a loud clang reverberates. We all jump, bubs included.

I am outraged. This, after all, is a labour recovery ward ... how stupid, how rude ... we're recovering, some consideration, some awareness of other people ...

You get the picture.

I look down at bubs, and after her initial shock, she's long let it go. In fact, there was no reaction. She's the one I'm concerned most about protecting, and she's golden. She got a fright and then she got over it. Daddy didn't.

You see what I mean?

You *know* what I mean – it's why you're reading this book. Your reactions mean you do and say stuff you regret, and this can go on for days, keeping you stuck in the past, preventing you sleeping, preventing you from enjoying this moment ...

Exhaustion just means it's so much harder to just watch your reaction, it's so much harder to maintain that half-step back.

Looking after your physical energy is one of the greatest things you can do to not be triggered in ways you regret. But exhaustion is part of a bigger cycle, one that also involves stress and how different parts of your brain think differently.

Out Of Your Mind

With the same event, why is it that sometimes you can respond magnificently and other times you react appallingly?

Stage fright – performance anxiety – is a great example, for sports people, musicians, public speakers, anyone taking an examination: you do it perfectly when no one's watching, but the day of the big event and everything falls apart, with your heart thumping and knees knocking. Fear sets in and you lose that free, fluid, spontaneous action.

The introduction of pressure creates a reaction that means you can't do what you've trained to do.

Or ... say you want to achieve a certain goal. Perhaps it's losing weight, getting your business off the ground, or learning a language.

You get set up, you learn all about how to get to your goal, you invest in a training programme and/or a coach so you know exactly what to do ... it's just that you don't do it.

Ever been in this situation?

Along with exhaustion, stress and pressure mean you are more likely to react in ways you wish you didn't. You may feel like you're out of your mind – and in many ways you're right. Understanding which part of your brain is kicking off can help enormously in dealing with your habitual reactions and doing things differently.

Animal or Human?

I'm going to give you a broad understanding of brain science and theory. I'm no expert, but a broad picture is all you need to understand what you need to move forward.

The brain is not a whole – it is made up of evolutionarily different parts. One of the oldest is sometimes called the reptilian brain. This is the part responsible for survival needs, and as such it is extraordinarily fast. It doesn't require conscious thought, it isn't cognitive, it is a pure reaction.

This part of the brain is about the "fight, flight or freeze" reactions. Aggression and avoidance you can probably understand, but freeze happens when you're up in front of a crowd and your brain turns to mush or when you're in *that* social situation and don't speak up for yourself.

It also is about the "feeding and fornicating" systems – I mention these because they all start with "F" and I think that's pretty cool. But also it explains the instant gratification response to stress and exhaustion that many have, in terms of launching into mindless feeding on junk food and/or fornication through useless one night stands and porn.

The second part we'll cover is the mammalian brain.

This is concerned with social connection and hierarchies. It's the part of you that is concerned with family links and what other people think about you.

This part of the brain is active, for example, if you find yourself feeling guilty for taking well deserved time out from your family for yourself; or if you find yourself "keeping the peace" with family members and others, even when they're creating you more work or even harming you.

It's also where fear of failure comes in.

Fear of failure is actually not about failure. It's all about the fear of failing in front of others – the fear of looking stupid. You can fail all you like in private and it doesn't matter so much, but the possibility of failing in front of people is a different kettle of fish. Right?

That social hierarchy focus then feeds the survival instinct. Fight, flight, freeze kicks in if your concern with other people is strong enough.

Perhaps you might see why you behave like you do in certain situations and around certain people?

The last part is the human brain – the evolved brain – which is about logic and reasoning. It's about self-realisation: goals and dreams.

This is the part of you that wants to become greater. But before you can take any steps towards more, you have to make sure, as coaching and learning specialist Dax Moy puts it, "the animals feel secure."

As he points out, their needs are different:

Reptile	Mammal	Human
Survive	Strive	Thrive
Stay the same	Stay the same	Wants change

You see the tension here? The different parts of your own brain need different things – and when active, these different parts of your brain will determine your behaviour:

Reaction	Response
Reptile/mammal	Human
Programme	Process
Instinct	Intellect
Immediate	Big picture
Fear-based	Dream-based
Threat-based	Possibility-based
Past/Future	Present/Future
Automatic/preverbal	Choice/reason

The Stress/Exhaustion Cycle of Doom

Stress (or threat) and exhaustion feed on each other. They combine to create an endless cycle. Stress is physically, mentally and emotionally draining. Exhaustion means you can't think clearly, you don't have perspective, you get overwhelmed and stressed more.

This cycle of doom means the reactive brain centres kick in much more easily. And since it's automatic, they bypass your reasoning centres. Sometimes you aren't even aware that you're doing something. You just act or do, and then the human brain regrets when it catches up.

The classic example is when you snap at your kids or partner – you don't mean to be like that, it's just they're *so* irritating – but really you're just knackered and can't think (or behave) straight.

Or when you're on a diet. Do you know when you break your diet? It's always from the afternoon onwards, when you get tired. You're fine in the morning, it's just when the afternoon energy slump comes around, you reach for the chocolate or the cake. Or it's last thing at night. You throw out your diet plan and reach for the Doritos, and beer, and gin and tonic, because, well, "you deserve it."

Same with one night stands and porn. That fornication response – quick and easy – kicks in later in the day. Surfing online porn is never something you get lost in first thing in the morning (unless you're seriously addicted) – and you're probably thinking a lot differently from the night before as you grab your shoes and try and sneak out of the bedroom before your ex-partner or other highly unsuitable person wakes up.[4]

---

[4] Alcohol? A little, as you know, calms the animals. More means they come out quicker, habitual reactions get bigger.

The animal brain just wants instant satisfaction, a quick fix: "Gimme comfort food," "Gimme release," or "I'm right, you're annoying, and here's why ... bam!"

Your emotions are affected in the same way. Feeling all over the place, emotionally? Depressed and low? You could just be chronically exhausted. You're just like a kid. A good night's rest helps everything.[5]

Thinking Humanly and Responding Consciously

What is the answer to stop acting from the animal brain, being so reactive and emotional?

The essential first step to getting free choice is that you tone down the stress and get enough rest.

Realise that if you want to be productive, getting overwhelmed and being stressed doesn't help you. Neither does doing things faster help you make clear decisions. Doing as much as possible will simply mean you're exhausted and unable to do anything tomorrow.

Sleep and quality rest is so crucial. You have to protect your energy and deal with your stress levels. Rest gives you clarity and awareness which gives you freedom of choice. Then you also can choose to respond in ways you want to so much easier, rather than reacting.

What's one of the most effective ways of not only getting deep rest and recharging and learning not to let situations overwhelm you? Meditation. I'll talk much more about this in Choice 6, but I thought I'd throw that in

---

[5] Not that this is the "cure all" for depression and bipolar and panic and all the rest, but sort out your exhaustion and, truly, everything is easier to deal with.

here so it can stew within you a little. Taking time out gives you so much back.

I know you're busy – you have a lot of responsibilities and little time. On the surface me telling you that you need to do less might not make a lot of sense.

But truly, you want and need effectiveness and enjoyment, not haste and stress. And that is what most people have – a cycle of overwhelm and struggle and exhaustion and reacting in ways they wish they didn't, or in ways that mean they never move forward.

It's the difference between being frantic, habitual and reactive or calm, conscious, and choosing your way through life. It's fundamental – this choice is everything. Perspective, the half-step back and awareness bring the freedom to respond as you wish.

CHAPTER ELEVEN

Choice 3: To Accept
(when you want to reject)

Acceptance Is It (There Is No Fourth Option)

Well known mindfulness and spiritual teacher Eckhart Tolle points out in his book *The Power of Now*, that in a situation you find intolerable, you have three options.

You could:

1. Change the situation

2. Leave the situation

3. Accept the situation

Commonly, people will say "I don't have a choice – I can't change or leave the situation." The truth is that you can, more than you realise. Just about always you can – it's that, actually, you don't *want* to.

For example, take a job that has become intolerable. I've heard countless people tell me they can't quit. The fact is they *can* quit – people quit their jobs all the time – it's just that they have too much invested in it. They *do* have a choice, it's just that, at the moment, they choose not to take it.

The same goes with a relationship: "I can't leave him or her." Actually, you could, it's just that getting untangled is something you're unprepared to do right now.

Seeing clearly that you always have a choice is taking responsibility for these situations. No one threw you into this – your past choices brought you here and, if you wish, you can get yourself out.

There's so much freedom right there.

Now, where you *clearly* cannot or do not wish to change or leave a situation you find intolerable, the third and only option left to you is full and complete acceptance.

You *must* accept. There are no other rational options.

However, instead of sucking it up and getting on with it, many people try and make a fourth option: resistance – complaining and whining and blaming and rejection and fighting.

Option four contains all stressful, pointless responses, leading to nothing but more stress. It keeps the problem at the forefront of your mind and, as what you focus on grows, it makes you a victim to the situation – it means you are choosing to be unhappy on an ongoing basis.

The joy and freedom of acceptance is seeing that, actually, what makes the intolerable is not the situation or person, but your attitude and thinking around it.

You can't always change the thing (especially in the short term), but you can certainly always change your attitude to it. Whether you want to or not is up to you.

Life becomes up to you; not them, *you* – and how wonderful is that?

Resistance and Why Acceptance Is the Best Foundation for Everything

Life is change.

Attempting to rigidly follow a set plan or idea, despite the reality of what is actually happening, will always be as fruitful and enjoyable as banging your head against a wall.

The cause of all your stress – *all stress* – is resisting what is.

Resistance is when your plan or idea meets an unmovable reality – and you keep pushing.

Take being stuck in traffic. Your plan is to get home by a certain time, but actually it's as soon as possible. There's idiots everywhere, going half the speed limit, Sunday driving and it's not even Sunday. Then you reach a traffic jam. Your knuckles grip the steering wheel tighter and tighter, you start yelling at everyone and anyone; your stress levels are through the roof.

The reality is that you can do nothing to get the traffic moving at your preferred speed. You could park the car and walk home – that's the change or leave option – but if you prefer not to walk, then you must accept the situation and adapt your original plan.

Traffic doesn't cause you stress.

Your fixation on "must get home" causes you stress. It is the resistance to the reality you are faced with that causes you stress.

You have a choice:

Stay stressed, hate every moment of the journey home, and when you get there be so wound up you can't even relax and enjoy having arrived.

Or you can stop the struggle, accept the reality of the situation, and get home at the same time (or faster, as you're less likely to cause an accident) and in a state of calmness and contentment. And you may have learned something along the way, because you tuned into a radio station, put a podcast on or had an audio book to hand.

Another example:

Lack of sleep causes a lot of people stress. But again – it's not the lack of sleep that is the problem, it's the fact that you're actively resisting the reality that you're awake.

You're totally focused on how exhausted you might feel in the morning if you stay awake any longer – and it's that mental activity and agitation that means you're so much less likely to fall asleep.

If you accept that reality is different from your plan, at least you'll be relaxed; sleep will come a whole lot easier when you don't fight being awake.

Do you know what I mean?

Get good at acceptance and we're not talking about stress management. We're talking about how life – your life – can be stress-*free*. Stress *can* be optional. Stress isn't about the thing, the circumstance, the person, it's completely about how you relate to it or them. That you can control.

The rational response to life, to all of life, as well as the end of all stress, lies in not rejecting and resisting, and instead accepting.

What Are You In Control Of?

> *"We make plans so God can laugh at them."*
>
> - Anon

You have an idea of how your goals and desires are going to be fulfilled. You have an idea of how your day is going to look. You have an idea of what should happen. But honestly – how often does life look *exactly* the way you want it to?

Very rarely. If it does, the nature of life is that it soon changes. Or, your mind being as it is, you get used to having that particular part of your picture in place and start focusing on what is missing.

You'll probably get stressed trying to make the conditions of life "just so," all so ultimately you can find satisfaction, be peaceful and happy.

Why not cut out the middle step? Be peaceful first – surrender to reality! Accept. Acknowledge you control very little. Stop fighting, stop resisting. If you value a peaceful, happy and effective life, there's no point in trying to fight reality. Start with what you are in control of: your attitude, what you focus on. Then, if you can and still want to, change the conditions you find yourself in.

The fact is the universe, God, reality or whatever greater power is actually in charge, often has a better, and definitely a bigger, idea. If you don't let go of your idea when the two don't match, it hurts as you struggle against what is happening. Resistance is futile.

You have no control over what happens. You can make a decision with a suggested plan and start heading in that direction, but be fluid to what happens next. Flexibility in your plans is everything. All you have total control over is your inner choice. Acceptance is the choice to prioritise your peace over everything else.

Choose To Not Give Up

Acceptance doesn't mean giving up your dreams. It means knowing that right now the path to your goal looks a little different than you expected.

Do you see the difference between *what is* happening and your idea of what *should be* happening?

The only time you have a problem is when you don't give up the "should."

When you come to terms with what is, when you fully accept it, all your suffering, all your stress goes away, immediately.

Then, and only then, you are able to work with what you have, rather than wishing for something else, or insisting that something else should be happening.

Give up the should and fully accept.

When you accept, you can see clearly; you can work with the facts as they are; you flow with what is; you're not causing yourself stress as you struggle against reality.

It's not about being a doormat – acceptance isn't about just taking that which is hurtful or damaging.

Complete acceptance also applies to your own innate wisdom and intuition. It means you do and say what you need to, in that moment.

A huge cause of internal strife is because you'll second guess what you really feel to do or say, simply because you don't trust yourself or have the courage to speak up for yourself. It'll take practice and awareness, like everything, but allow yourself to do and be and say whatever you wish. As long as your intention is to build and not to hurt, you cannot go wrong.

The whole universe responds to someone who, in the words of the serenity prayer, has the courage to change the things they can change, the serenity to accept the things they can't, and the wisdom to know the difference.

> *"Accept – then act. Whatever the present moment contains, accept it as if you have chosen it. Always work with it, not against it."*
>
> - Eckhart Tolle, spiritual teacher

Choose Not To Push – Get Fluid

> *"Happiness and freedom begin with a clear understanding of one principle: Some things are within our control, and some things are not. It is only after you have faced up to this fundamental rule and learned to distinguish between what you can and can't control that inner tranquility and outer effectiveness become possible."*
>
> - Epictetus, Greek philosopher

Stop pushing. Pushing doesn't get you what you want, only what you don't want. You think you are in control. You strive and force and try, and for what? A life of struggle? Is that how you want to live?

No, of course not. It's just often you don't realise how much you push.

Nothing happens for pushy people. Really, it doesn't. They just make life difficult for everyone around them, including themselves.

Some might say that "the squeaky wheel gets the oil" – the ones that complain get the attention. But in my experience, the most help goes to those who politely, easily and consistently ask for it, working with what they have and not insisting on having something they don't.

Life is meant to be one of ease. Don't get me wrong – life still involves action – but action that is inspired, fluid and simple.

All the great things that have come to you have come with this straightforward, flowing effortlessness. A moment of inspiration or intuition and then an outpouring. Absorption in presence and then simple, obvious action follows.

Instinct, Flow, the Zone, Grace.

Every good thing has come this way – and it doesn't matter if you are an athlete, an artist, a writer, a mechanic, a father, a teacher or a business woman.

You act and you choose and you do, but the best comes when you work with the present, not against it; when you let go of the future – of any idea of what *should* result from your actions; when you are fluid and absorbed.

The greatest moments have always come from this total presence. Not overly concerned with the result or the plan, simply doing the right thing to do as it felt in that moment.

Control is the direct opposite. It kills inspiration and grace. It kills effortlessness and fluidity.

When you control, you struggle and you try and you strain.

Struggle and stress happen when you think you know what you need to do, and it's not happening according to your plan.

Instead of being fluid, you push a little more, and a little more. The resistance gets bigger and bigger. You get more and more exhausted, more and more stressed. There's less and less enjoyment.

That beautiful state of fluidity dies when you are resisting what is, when you're not accepting. Learning to be aware of when struggle comes in and – knowing it is counter-productive – simply letting go, is one of the greatest habits you can form.

Letting go of control is that simple. Let any form of struggling be an indicator of control so you can simply stop. Stop fighting. Stop resisting what is.

The bottom line is: protect your own peace. Protect the baseline.

You think you can do that?

Of course you can. Just now, notice the trying and let it go. That is all. Little by little. Be present, be calm – just for now. Choose to accept, not reject.

Accept Everything, Resist Nothing

Practising acceptance is simple.

Try something with me. Become aware of how you are in your body. Be aware of any tensions, emotions, annoyances, thoughts. Be aware of everything there.

Now – be 100% okay with everything that is going on, as it is. Don't try and change a single thing. Just for this moment, be present to everything. Settle in, stop the fight, drop the tension.

Accept everything, resist nothing. See how perhaps your mind wants something different; don't bite. Allow everything as it is right now. Totally stop any controlling and simply be with all that is happening.

Give yourself permission to relax, to let go. Take a deep breath. Take another. How does it feel to accept and allow? How does it feel to stop "doing," stop changing and trying, just for this moment? Pretty good, right?

Emotional Freedom From Pain

Complete non-resistance is also the answer to any problems with intense emotions or physical pain. Suffering is not actually caused by emotion or pain, but by your active resistance to it. You don't want to experience intensity. You're scared of what might happen, so you try to push it away.

Do you recall that, chemically speaking, emotions only last 90 seconds?

By completely and absolutely allowing the experience, without labelling it wrong or right, without trying to change it or push it away, you will find it flows through very quickly. Breathe deep. Try not to get caught up in it: witness it, observe it, be with it. You will find intensity is not something to be scared of. You *can* handle it.

It may be uncomfortable, this is true – but the degree of discomfort is directly related to how much you resist it.

If you truly witness it, you will find that you are not the emotion. It is there, you experience it, but it's not you, it doesn't define you. You are something else.

Emotion just needs to move. The less you take it personally as something that is inherently "you" and just let it move, the more quickly and appropriately it will come out. When I stuffed my emotions down they only exploded in ways I regretted later.

It's never the experience, your suffering lies in the resistance to it.

Pain and Your Story

Similarly, physical pain may not be pleasant, but it is made far worse by the frustrations, the tensions, the fear, the projections into the future that you entertain; in other words, the "story" around the pain.

Your story creates a whole future scenario to the pain you're experiencing now. Anticipating this future creates a whole new level of tension and resistance to the pain.

It is the ongoing "checking in," the examining, the prodding, the constant attempts to relieve the pain that creates more suffering than the simple fact of the pain itself.

You know this already.

If you've ever given birth or if you've ever moved through the pain that comes with exercise, you will know that the body can continue long after the mind has had enough.

Your story and mental processing causes the suffering, not the experience itself. Coping with pain is a mind game.

I'm not saying don't do anything. I'm not saying don't do the things that you can do to relieve or get help for pain. When I had a headache, I used to actively try and deal with it on the level of the mind alone. How silly. So much simpler and quicker to take a couple of aspirin and get on with the fact of living.

Accept it all, resist nothing.

Practical Ways of Ending Resistance To Pain

There are a few practical techniques you can use to end resistance and let go into acceptance – you will prefer one to another, of course.

The first, and a good fall back, will always be to give full awareness to the physical or emotional pain without getting lost in your story and the thinking about it.

Fully notice it, without judgement. Sink into the middle of the intensity. Be with it, be curious, be interested. Take some deep breaths if you need to. You can try breathing as if you were inhaling and exhaling into and out of the site of the pain. Even emotional pain can be located somewhere on a physical level. But always recognise the difference between being fully present with it and thinking about it – that is key.

Or, you can tune in and give the pain an exact location, as well as giving it a colour, and a rating of intensity from 1-10. Stay with it and be curious if the pain changes in any of these. As you settle down, resisting less and accepting more, you will find they do change.

Another tip is to actively change the way you think and talk about the pain. Get good at acceptance and you will recognise this anyway, but start now and see that you aren't depressed or in pain or anxious, but that you *have* depression, or you *have* pain, or you *have* anxiety. This will help you in realising that you are not your pain, you are not the emotion; it is not inherently you. If you are not it, then already there's a half-step back from it, there's awareness.

Or, some people like to throw open their arms and exclaim, out loud, "Bring it on!" How can you resist anything when you have that kind of attitude? Similarly, others like to picture themselves opening an inner door and welcoming in the pain. "Sit down, you are welcome here too," they will say. Resistance and welcoming are two different attitudes, aren't they?

In a similar vein is practising gratitude. Actively speak and be grateful for your body, for your life, even for the pain. It's a seemingly bizarre tip, but it really works.

You see, resistance is always caused by the focus on what is wrong. Gratitude is the direct opposite. In resistance there is a struggle and a fight, even on a physical level. Everything gets tight and tense which causes more pain. When you are thankful, the fight or flight response is switched off, the body itself relaxes and tension decreases, as does the pain.

It's acceptance through shifting your attention – and the great thing is the body doesn't know the difference between spontaneous gratitude that arises when something nice happens to you, and you choosing to be thankful. But as studies are starting to show, your body definitely responds. I'll talk a lot more about gratitude in the next chapter.

Whatever you do, the key is to always give your full attention to what you are doing. A common "mistake" is to have half an eye on acceptance and half an eye on the pain; "Is it gone yet?"

Do it with 100%: be 100% okay with whatever is happening. Seek not to change a thing; ironically (to your mind), if it's going to change, it will change when you fully and completely accept it.

Freedom from pain comes from a level of acceptance where you don't care if the pain is still there or not. You aren't accepting in order to get rid of it – that's not full acceptance.

The greatest lesson pain will give you is complete acceptance.

If you can come to terms with emotional and physical pain, it has no hold on you anymore. You are free with it. And, perhaps even greater, is that you can accept anything, you can be free from *any* suffering. As the former pro-cyclist Lance Armstrong said after cancer and chemotherapy:

> *"I take nothing for granted.*
> *I now have only good days, or great days."*

Mastering acceptance and becoming a living embodiment of a choice for peace – no matter "the facts" of your past and present reality – what a wonderful service that is to anyone struggling. By overcoming your suffering, you give hope to everyone you come in contact with, because you're living from the experience and not just an idea about it.

Regret and Guilt

One thing that will stop you accepting anything is regret. Another is guilt.

These two feelings mean you won't want to acknowledge the pain at all. Instead you'll do everything you can to repress it and distract, even sedate, yourself. Unfortunately, the more you do this, the more the pain will push back – a little like trying to hold a beach ball down underwater. You can get away with it for a little while, but it takes all of your energy, and when the ball finally escapes it comes to the surface with some power.

The other side of regret and guilt is feeling that you have to suffer for what you believe you have done. You deserve this, you need to atone, you need to revisit and revisit and recycle how wrong you were, how bad you are.

I'm no psychologist and, at the risk of reducing what is perhaps a complex state of affairs, what you most likely need to do is come to terms with your past, and let the beach ball go. Talking to someone you trust can be incredibly freeing. Unfortunately, regret and guilt – pride too – may mean it seems incredibly difficult to open up to anyone.

But you aren't the first and you won't be the last to go through whatever you're going through. There are people who know exactly what it's like; even if you believe you're the only one. There is a way out, and sometimes you have to go through it (without reinforcing your story) in order to go beyond it.

Perhaps just knowing this may make it easier. Perhaps looking at why this is happening *for* you, not to you, will help. Perhaps just knowing that you're going through this so you can help others may make it easier.

All I know, from personal experience, is that there is a way out – there is, always.

Faith and Trust

"Good morning, this is God. I will be handling all your problems
today. I will not need your help, so relax and have a good day!"

- Anon

Letting go in acceptance, knowing that you can afford to stop controlling and seeking to secure everything, may require faith or trust. But here's the thing: you only have to accept right now. You only have to release your controlling grip on your life as it is just now, just in this moment.

Take an honest look. There is very little you actually have to attend to, right now. See what happens if you do let go – just for this moment. Apart from the initial courage to make a different choice, you'll find it's quite easy. It's actually very peaceful to not be in charge, to release the grip, to not worry for once.

If you always do what you have always done, you will get what you have always got.

If you want more peace, peace that lasts, if you want an end to suffering, forever, then you need to try something a little radical. You'll find that if you actually do, one day you will look back and wonder how you ever lived any other way.

CHAPTER TWELVE

Choice 4: To Appreciate
(when you want to criticise)

"Men are disturbed not by the things that happen,
but by the opinion of the things."

- Epictetus, Greek philosopher

Choose Your Attitude – the Glass Half-Full

The necessary counterpart to acceptance is choosing your attitude.

Since sometimes you can't (or won't) change or leave a situation, you must change your reaction to it – so you accept. But you can also change your attitude to any situation as well.

Your attitude is key in unlocking every situation in life.

Choosing a different attitude is a small shift in perspective, but it has a huge effect in terms of your enjoyment and effectiveness in life.

It is a simple choice to see the glass as half-full. It takes so little to make that choice. But it changes everything.

Focus on what you want to grow, because indeed, what you focus on does grow. What you expect to see, you will see. This was beautifully put by a wise teacher some time ago: what you sow is what you reap. Jesus wasn't talking about potatoes.

Look for goodness and love from the world and that's exactly what you find. Expect the world to be a fearful place where you need to fight to get what you need and that's exactly what you get.

You focus on the negativity, on what is missing, on what is wrong and that is what is magnified. Focus on the good, on the opportunities, on what you do have and that is what blossoms.

A life of joy and ease or sorrow and hardship is your choice. It all has its basis in your attitude and what you put your attention on. Your attitude is the foundation of your life.

Let the glass be half-full, always.

The Silver Lining

There is always a silver lining to any – and every – situation, even the most challenging.

A choice to see the glass as half-full means you take charge. It means you don't let the situation define you; you define the situation.

It matters not where you find yourself. In fact, the more challenging the situation, the more important it is to focus on the silver lining.

There's the famous story of James Stockdale, a US Navy pilot held prisoner during the Vietnam war for seven years in appalling conditions, including regular torture. It's a stand out tale from Jim Collins's book,

Good to Great. Stockdale spoke about his attitude during the time:

> *"I never doubted not only that I would get out, but also that I would prevail in the end and turn the experience into the defining event of my life, which, in retrospect, I would not trade."*

It's important to note that James Stockdale wasn't a head-in-the-sand optimist.

In fact, when asked about those who didn't survive, he tagged them "the optimists" – those that were solely focused on a future goal without any acceptance of the realities of the present moment. He said they died of broken hearts.

Stockdale put extreme importance on seeing clearly the reality of your situation based on full and frank acceptance of it:

> *"This is a very important lesson. You must never confuse faith that you will prevail in the end – which you can never afford to lose – with the discipline to confront the most brutal facts of your current reality, whatever they might be."*

A goal, an optimism, an attitude of holding to the silver lining is essential – but it goes hand-in-hand with acceptance. A winning combination when mastered, this enables you to make the most of any and every situation.

Thrive or Die?

Whether you thrive or die in any situation is not dependent on the circumstances.

The difference between a setback and an opportunity will always be your perspective on it.

One perspective is constrictive: it focuses on the wrong, on what you can't do. It reduces your choice: it means things get heavy; it decreases your power to play. You abandon self-responsibility and enter and carry a victim mentality: "Poor me."

The other perspective is expansive: it focuses on what you have and what you can do next. It maximises your choices; it brings light, hope and excitement; it increases your power to play in the game you find yourself in.

Do you see the difference?

Even, and especially, in the most challenging times, take the responsibility to make it about what you can gain from the situation. Even if it's a simple question of examining "What did I learn from this? What will I do differently next time?", you can turn everything into an advantage for you.

I know it can be tough at times, but be smart. Keep coming back to focus on the good, even the smallest, simplest things.

Stress is always reacting negatively to what is: "This should not be happening to me!" It focuses on what is wrong. It denies the reality of the situation.

The fact is it is happening to you. Choose to accept; then choose your attitude.

Flip any negativity over and focus on a silver lining. You may never know the "why" of a situation, as in "Why is this happening to me?", but certainly you'll know what you can learn from it – if you choose to stop resisting and look.

Don't let the situation define you. It never needs to.

You get to define what "success" is, what the silver lining is to you. When you define the situation, you get to play on your terms.

Appreciation Versus Condemnation

> *"What can everyone do? Praise and blame.*
> *This is human virtue, this is human madness."*
>
> - Friedrich Nietzsche, German philosopher

Choosing to see the glass as half-full is a simple choice in attitude or in perspective.

Practically speaking it is the simple act of appreciation. Appreciation is the simple choice to approve, to see the good around you.

It instantly changes your mood, the biochemical makeup of your brain. You join an upward spiral. The more you do, the better you feel, so the more you do it. Appreciation is the direct opposite to condemnation or judgement, which is downward spiralling.

Since your awareness is creative, what you put your attention on grows in significance. No matter the circumstances or the person, you can always find something to appreciate. The more you appreciate, the more you find to appreciate.

If you want a downward spiral of stress, negativity, overwhelm, anger and frustration to grow in your life, taking you further and further down into misery, then actively practise criticism, judgement and condemnation.

The more you do this, the more you'll enjoy misery and suffering. You're training yourself to dwell in the negative, and that is dodgy ground you're preparing. If you like feeling depressed and angry and anxious, keep doing it. The health of your whole mindset has its roots right here.

You see – you choose to get overwhelmed and negative when you choose to focus on what is wrong so much that you can't see what is good and right. Negativity (boosted by exhaustion) removes your clarity so that you can't see any alternative; that is your life – a deep dark hole.

It's not really, it's just the mindset you've carefully prepared over the years.

Any stress is never about the thing – it is always about your reaction to the thing. The end of all stress lies in not focusing on what is wrong, instead it stems from focusing on what is good – choosing to appreciate.

Choosing to appreciate is not sticking your head in the sand and avoiding the things that you have to deal with.

Acceptance and then choosing to appreciate is taking a half-step back from what you don't like and giving yourself another perspective. Your problem is still there, but it's not the only thing you see; it doesn't exhaust your attention.

It's not an either/or choice – you can be calm and still have a problem. But in that perspective there is more choice; there is freedom to move; there is creativity. When you're solely focused on what you don't like, that's all there is.

Choose to appreciate. It instantly makes your world bigger. It changes everything. It makes your life so much better – all because you're responsible for defining your world.

Appreciation and Praise

The smallest choices consistently made – day in, day out – have the biggest impact.

Practising appreciation is one of these. It turns a glass half-full choice into a habit, a permanent way of seeing and living.

Appreciation is a mental choice: "Yes, that is good, yes, I approve of that," but it is also essential to make it an action, as in speaking out this approval and appreciation.

That can be as simple as sharing with another how good you think something is: "Isn't this view particularly amazing?" or praising the person: "I really appreciate how you make me tea every afternoon," "You are so efficient with your work for me," "Looking exceptionally sharp this morning" ...

You get the idea ... but if you are a typical human, you just don't praise others. You don't take the time to appreciate out loud.

If you realised the power of appreciation – to you personally – you would fill your days with praise. It's a shame because this is where you start taking other people for granted – and that is a very slippery slope we'll talk about shortly.

Do it now – stop and find something to appreciate in this moment. Anything, big or small. Then find something to praise about a person. Say it to them. Don't stop – do both of these things as often as you can.

Notice judgement as it comes up, because it will – become alert to those times when you want to come in with judgement and condemnation. See if you can switch it around and find the good there. This doesn't mean you stop correcting or giving feedback to others, it just means you're doing it from a different place. Just do it.

You don't have to put on a different manner; be yourself, just the appreciative version of yourself. Make praise your own. Be you, but be active in your praise and appreciation.

Try it. It's one of the greatest things you can do to make your romantic relationship better, stronger, more loving – and you know what that means. Making sure the fire in your relationship never goes out can be as simple as making your praise and appreciation a daily practice.

Right now, make the choice to see what is good in your life and in your world. Choose for an upward, expansive direction to life as opposed to one that takes you down, that makes life smaller.

Constantly, speak and do and be appreciation. Be very careful of condemnation. Find as many ways as possible to praise the people in your life. Just do it and see what happens.

Gratitude

"Gratitude unlocks the fullness of life. It turns what we have into enough, and more. It turns denial into acceptance, chaos to order, confusion to clarity. It can turn a meal into a feast, a house into a home, a stranger into a friend ... Gratitude makes sense of our past, brings peace for today, and creates a vision for tomorrow."

- Melody Beattie, author

Gratitude naturally flows from appreciation. You make the choice to appreciate something or someone and gratitude is the result. The more you do, the more you get. Gratitude, like praise, is also very creative.

Gratitude is so simple and powerful, but it is rarely done because we aren't aware of its importance. It is one of the most crucial choices you can make simply because it solves one of your biggest problems:

You take so much of your life for granted.

You ignore the goodness that is already here. That you are alive, that your body, as a whole, is healthy and generally does what you want it to do, that you have a roof over your head, a shirt on your back, that you have people you love.

The poverty of the so-called first world doesn't lie in a poverty of possessions, but in the lack of the recognition of how good your life is, exactly as it is, right now.

You have so much and you don't even see it, you're not aware of huge chunks of it.

A perfect example landed in my lap a few months ago when my computer died. Completely kaput.

Funny how I can use something every day and not really notice how much a part of my life it has become until it is no longer there.

You ever notice that?

How something can be essential in your life and yet you only truly appreciate it when it's gone? It's sad but true. You do it with things, you do it with people, you do it with your own body, with your health. You only appreciate how good you had it when it's no longer there.

Gratitude is the answer – if you want an end to missing out, if you want to make sure you make the most of what you have.

One of the most inspiring stories I have ever heard regards Martine Wright, a woman who lost her legs in one of the "7/7" terrorist bomb attacks on the London Underground. Years later she was interviewed and what struck me was her attitude.

In the interview, Wright says she considers herself lucky, lucky she didn't die. Not only that, she describes losing her legs as the "most life-changing thing that has had such profound and positive effects." She continues:

> *"It may sound absolutely mad to say that ... But my life now is so amazing. I've had the opportunity to do so much, meet so many people. I don't think I would turn that clock back if I had the chance ...*
>
> *I've had my days of saying 'why me?', believe me. But ... I've dealt with it. I've got new legs, not no legs. Anything is possible."*[6]

Isn't that incredible? Her overwhelming response is one of gratitude and possibility. Her focus is not on the legs that she has lost but the fact that she is still alive, and all the good that has, and will, come from that.

Sometimes losing something can be a wake-up call. It can shift your attention from merely getting through life to truly living. It can move your focus from what you don't have to what you do have. It can show you that there's no time for indifference, that life itself is an incredible gift.

---

[6] After the bomb, Wright had gone on to become captain of the British Paralympic Sitting volleyball team and a TV sports reporter. She was awarded an MBE for services to sport in 2016. For more of her story, see her book, *Unbroken*.

However! You don't *need* to lose anything to take your life to a whole different level – let this be your wake-up call.

So many people don't realise how truly rich they are. They have so much, and yet they don't realise it simply because they take big chunks of their life for granted.

I had an ear infection not so long ago, meaning I had no balance. Even the act of sitting up in bed and getting to the bathroom was a major achievement. As the infection left, how sweet was it to walk freely? Very.

I can't tell you how powerful the simple act of being grateful is. Going out of your way to be thankful transforms your attitude to life. The simple fact that you are alive becomes a source of richness and wonder.

Find as many ways as you can to express your gratitude. Be thankful. Just try it.

Don't Wait To Feel It

Many people will hear what I have to say on being active with appreciation and gratitude and reply, "Well, I'll appreciate someone when I feel it, otherwise it's just fake."

Are you one of them? It's okay, but honestly – do you think that?

Trouble is, by waiting to feel it before you do it, you've got it all back to front.

You can wait a very long time to feel something. Feelings are pretty random in terms of you never know when they will come and go. But if you'd like to create your future ahead of you, if you want freedom of choice, if you want not only greater joy but greater effectiveness, if you want to be bulletproof to stress and negativity, if you want to really and truly be Alive?

Get it the right way around: your thoughts create the foundation for your feelings – if they come at all.

Choose to think and say appreciation and gratitude because *then* you'll feel it. The thoughts you choose to focus on and cultivate through your words and actions give rise to your feelings. Don't wait – think and act, then you get the good vibes.

"I Don't Need To, I'm Good ..."

Believe that "Life is fine right now so I don't need to ..."?

You feel like you're wandering along fine just now, but what if things change? What if something goes unexpected or wrong? What then? Do you have the resources to cope, and remain calm and unruffled if it hits the fan?

I met a guy recently who was re-sitting an Armed Forces meditation/mindfulness/200% of life course I run for bomb disposal experts. The first time through I could tell he was just along for the ride – nice guy, super funny, but it just didn't interest him in any way.

He returned for a second go because weeks after the first course he was diagnosed with Parkinson's. Boom. In his 40s and suddenly, out of the blue, faced with his own mortality.

His mind now wasn't his friend – he saw exactly how he needed to get to master his own choices, and quickly.

What if you, like many people do, wake up one morning sliding into misery, suffering and struggling, anxious and overwhelmed with seemingly no way out?

What then?

It happens. You were never depressed or anxious or manic before, but all of a sudden it seems like it jumps on you. It can be triggered by events, but sometimes it can just happen. The Curse of the Pretty Good Life we were talking about earlier means you have no resources, no ability to choose your way through the mine-field your mind can become so rapidly and unexpectedly.

Often we have no resilience – no ability to focus on the positive when we most need it – because we didn't practise it when the going was good, when it was easy to do so.

It's like turning up for a race without doing any training, thinking, "I'll get fitter as I do it." It's like showing up for a public performance without practising, "When the pressure is on, I'll step up."

That there is the hard way to do anything.

Do it now while it's easy, then you'll be so much more resilient to the tough times. The fact is you will get so resilient you might not even notice events you would have formerly found tough; you've become "mega-good."

You think life is "fine" now? Would you like it to be better? Practising means you'll step up to a whole new realm of good, and that really is a fine place to be in.

Criticism and Honesty

Now, you may say: "I'm telling the truth ... I'm calling it as it is, being honest – I don't want to live life any other way."

I'm not saying to lie. I'm not saying to stop being honest and true to yourself.

However –

What many people call "honesty" is often an excuse to slam other people – to make yourself feel better, to prevent you from opening up and/or to keep others at arm's length, to appear to be in control when actually you're more confused or unsure of yourself than ever.

"Honesty" is also often the hallmark of the fanatic, the Zealot.

Zealotry – I'm right and you're wrong because you're different from me – is regularly seen in any new convert to any belief system. This includes *any* beliefs that you may hold dear, not just religious beliefs – politics, veganism, the *Star Wars* films. A quick search of the internet will show you how ridiculous people can get about their beliefs: I need to be right, so I'll make you wrong.

Zealotry only fades and wisdom blooms when you become secure enough in your own self and your own path that you can allow others to live and be different from you.

To be accepting of a difference in opinion or lifestyle, to let someone make their own choices, to not need to make someone else wrong in order for you to be right takes a huge amount of personal security and humility on your behalf.

So be careful – "honesty" can mean you're not that secure, you're not as sure as you think you are. Because if you were, there is no need for your opinion.

When a Spade Is a Club

If you're constantly being "honest" and "calling a spade a spade" yet unable to find anything good in a situation or about a person, it's an excellent sign you're way out of balance. Your "honesty" is hurting you and your experience of life.

I remember listening to the Dalai Lama being interviewed on the radio when the interviewer asked him about his relationship with the Chinese leader. I really sat up at that point, as this is the man who has burnt down the Dalai Lama's monasteries, killed his monks, stolen his country and meant he's had to flee to India – it made my petty grudges at the time look tiny.

"The Chinese leader has taught me a lot about patience," the Dalai Lama replied – at which point I almost fell off my chair. I thought if there was anyone who had a *right* to a grudge, a *right* to complain, a *right* to be honest, it would be the Dalai Lama.

It was then I saw he was playing a much bigger game, a game I was only just becoming aware of: the game of 200% – a game based on full and complete responsibility for everything that happens in life, responding not reacting, and finding the silver lining in everything.

He saw, without doubt, that all of his choices affected him directly. Criticism and condemnation – even when it seems valid – bites you hardest. It means you are actually reinforcing judgement, the negative, and your focus on what is wrong within you and your life.

That in turn shrinks your universe, makes you a victim, removes choice, makes stress and resentment and anger and reaction and suffering much simpler to unconsciously fall into, and it means the other person is always to blame.

Appreciation, even just of what you have personally learned from a situation or person, is about responsibility. It makes you strong, resilient, flexible, happier, and grudge-free.

How To Be Honest Without Being Angry

This does not mean you don't speak. It doesn't mean you don't say what you'd like to see happen to someone who is affecting you. It does not mean you don't help someone see something they can do better or help them realise the consequences of their choices. How can any of us learn anything without feedback?

Those times you need to speak up, you speak up.

I have personally lost far too much time and wasted so much energy by *not* speaking up, not saying what I needed to say, and then having it eat me up for days after. It's all about low self-esteem and a belief that you're wrong and they're right. It's also, perversely, about wanting to be right so much that you're unprepared to open your mouth and appear wrong.

I would see this person later and always be seething internally. I couldn't be innocent and fresh with them, I always wanted to punch them in the face; and it was all my problem.

Speaking your truth and being honest is necessary – carrying grudges kills you. It is also a fine art. Do it in a timely manner so you don't waste life by dwelling on it for too long, and do it with zero attachment to them "getting it."

You just have to open your mouth and speak. It may feel like it has a roar, but the sooner you do it, the "cleaner" and less distorted by anger it will be. The more you do this, the better you get at it too. It's a skill, it takes practice.

Being invested in them getting it and doing anything different is always a recipe for personal disaster.

They may, they may not – but your peace and happiness is then linked directly to them changing. Linking your peace and happiness to anything on the outside is always the opposite of freedom and independence. You're back on the rollercoaster with no way to get off.

It also means you are unconsciously focused on what you think is wrong with people. When they change – ah, well now I can accept you. Until then? I just want to punch you in the face until you get it.

The bottom line for all of this is: "Do you want to be right? Or do you want to be happy?"

You say your piece, and then you let go. Sometimes it's obvious they haven't heard a single word you said. The only reason you would continue to bang on about what you want them to do is that you want to be right, you want them to change.

So many relationships are based on this attempt to control someone else.

When Do People Hear You?

In their own good time. But they are much more likely to hear you if they feel a foundation of acceptance and appreciation from you.

What distinctly counts is your attitude: "Am I trying to build or destroy?" "Am I seeing the glass half-full or half-empty?" and "Am I unconditional in my giving?" – do you *need* them to do what you say?

Appreciation, acceptance and allowance gives space for transformation. Condemnation and judgement is confining and restricting.

How do you feel when someone judges or harshly criticises you? Do you feel like co-operating with them?

No, you don't. But when someone makes you feel accepted, okay exactly as you are, it's a whole different feeling, isn't it? One approach is restrictive, the other nurturing. You want to push the first people away, you want to pull the second in closer.

The whole universe works in the same way. A foundation in acceptance and appreciation invites growth, natural growth. A foundation in control and condemnation results in limitation and confinement.

Acceptance openly invites; judgement narrowly defines.

Overwhelm and the Future Gap

So enough about other people – back to you.

Do you know what the answer to being stressed and overwhelmed is? I'm sure you do, by now – it's about your choice to put your attention *either* on what is wrong and what is missing *or* on the gift, the silver lining, on what you're grateful for.

But here's a crucial understanding that will really help you get to grips with your own overwhelm. Especially if you're a regular goal-setter, an ambitious sort or perfectionist, someone who entertains serious expectations about themselves, about what they "should" be able to do or be.

Overwhelm always comes in when you're focused on the difference between where you want to be – a future goal – and where you are, right now.

The bigger the difference, the bigger the overwhelm: "I have so much to do, and so little time to do it."

You indulge in this difference, what life and business coach Paul Mort calls "the future gap," and overwhelm sets in. Overwhelm begets negativity and self-doubt; you start to spin around in little circles, going nowhere fast. Procrastination, avoidance and even straight up self-sabotage come along for the ride too.

Regardless of what you want, where are you now? Where have you come from?

Overwhelm is mastered when you stop trying to be in the future already. You can anchor yourself further in a sense of achievement or improvement when you look back and examine how far you've come.

Writing a gratitude list, or as Paul Mort more precisely puts it, a list of "wins" – successes and achievements and lessons – at the end of the day may help you base yourself on what is right: what you *have* done, what you have learnt, and what your next steps are.

Do you see how powerful that is in giving yourself solid ground to move forward from, as opposed to focusing on the gap, on what is missing?

Shame And The Past

If you are ashamed of a past action, this is a good sign. Really. You have already learnt something, you are already on the road to behaving differently – otherwise you wouldn't see it, you wouldn't be ashamed.

The question now is whether you'll take steps so that you consciously choose your behaviour next time, or whether you allow yourself to stay unconscious and choose to follow the same reaction again, and again.

Is your current shame enough to take steps to overcome the pain of change so you can live in a way that means you never feel that shame and guilt again?

Anxiety And The Future

Anxious for an unknown future? Here's a further practice for you. Maharishi, my Bright Path Ishaya teacher told me this one, and it works beautifully – if you do it fully.

Simply be grateful now for the future moment you're concerned about. Rest and be thankful now, secure and stable in the knowledge, even the assumption, that the future turns out in the best possible way for you.

It will require you to stop thinking about the future and the gap, and get a solid foundation in present moment gratitude. Obviously, the more you practise appreciation and gratitude, the stronger your ability will be to simply be grateful, now.

But when you notice you're slipping back into concern and anxiety, simply and fully come back to this gratitude that the future will turn out just perfectly. Job done.

The fact is, if you embrace full and complete responsibility for all of your life, the future has always turned out perfectly for you. Here you are because everything in the past has brought you here.

You can focus on what went wrong, or you can focus on what you got right, what you learnt, what you now have.

Anxiety, shame, overwhelm, negativity are all incredibly weakening. Gratitude is the strongest foundation for every part of your life now, and moving forward.

See What You Do Have

> *"Be content in what you have, rejoice in the way things are.*
> *When you realise there is nothing lacking,*
> *the whole world belongs to you."*
>
> - Lao Tzu, Chinese philosopher

The greatest thing about appreciation and the resulting gratitude is that the more you give it, the more you appreciate how truly great your life and the world is, exactly as it is. Each moment starts genuinely being experienced as perfect, needing nothing. You can fully enjoy each and every moment as it is given to you.

Many say at this point, "What about reality, the 'actual' state of my life, my community, the world? There is so much obviously wrong, and so much to be fixed. There's nothing perfect about it."

Put that to one side, just for a moment.

Instead, appreciate and be grateful for everything that you *personally* have right now. Leave the past for what it is; gone. Don't worry about the future and what your mind believes you perhaps might not have. Give yourself completely to this moment and see what you do have, right now.

When you completely "let go" in this moment with appreciation and gratitude, you will find you have everything you personally need, for now. In fact, you actually have so much that you totally take for granted, simply because of the mind's habit of looking for what you don't have.

Recognise that part of your mind will always look for what is wrong. It is never satisfied. You have strengthened it over the years and so no matter how much you have, it will always look for, and find, what you don't. There are a lot of stressed, unhappy rich people out there.

Focusing on lack causes you stress. The habit of leaving this moment causes you stress. Being stressed means you cannot effectively, or enjoyably, help yourself, let alone anyone else.

Holding tight to your plan – your idea of the way you think it should look – also causes you stress. It also means you cannot see with clarity and perspective; you can only see your idea.

Richard Bach, author of *Johnathan Livingston Seagull*, once wrote:

> "What the caterpillar calls the end of the world,
> the master calls a butterfly."

There perhaps is a perfection at play – a silver lining – you cannot see until you drop the focus on what is wrong. Until you look calmly, with innocence, you won't know.

See what is beyond the limitations of your mind and you *will* experience the absolute perfection of this moment. Help yourself first before you try and fix the world. End stress by conquering the habits of your mind and you will be able to truly give to others, you will be able to bring lasting change – and all with a big smile:

> *"If you want to awaken all of humanity, then awaken all of yourself.*
> *If you want to eliminate the suffering in the world, then eliminate all*
> *that is dark and negative in yourself. Truly, the greatest gift you have*
> *to give is that of your own self-transformation."*

- Wang Fou, Chinese philosopher

Radical Appreciation

> *"We are not here to change the world,*
> *we are here to love it."*

- Anthony de Mello, Jesuit priest and spiritual teacher

Stick with me for this one. What if … what if the foundation for solving the problems of the world lay in how you – yes, you – thought about it?

There is the much used quote, often attributed to scientist Albert Einstein:

> *"No problem can be solved by the same kind of thinking that created it."*

It could be that forming an outlook based in acceptance, appreciation and seeing the glass as half-full is the single most creative and useful choice you could master – for yourself and the entire world.

Maharishi Sadashiva Isham, the teacher of my Bright Path Ishaya teacher once said:

> *"The simple guiding principle here is this: if we are sowing division, preaching destruction, seeking or finding evil in the world (even if we are looking for it with the intention of removing it!), then we are part of the problem, not the cure."*

The problem doesn't lie in the obvious problems of your life or the world. It is that the human brain constantly looks for – and finds – them. Your mind creates problems often out of nothing at all.

It is the defining of evil, of judgement itself that is at the core of all separation, all misunderstanding, all the world's troubles. It is the dividing of the world into us and them, the familiar and the strange, the righteous and the blasphemers. In the Judeo-Christian tradition, weren't the first humans only removed from the perfection of the Garden of Eden when they indulged in the knowledge of good and evil – when they came to know judgement?

I know this might be a hard pill to swallow – and I'm being deliberately "spiritual" on this – but consider this idea for a moment:

> *What if your attention could become so devoted to praise, gratitude and love, that nothing else could exist in your presence?*

What if? The rememberings of the great masters of this world all whisper this promise. Our legends and stories throughout time are thick with the power of love to transform monsters into angels, to lift the veil, to allow freedom – for all.

What if?

And how are you going to know unless you do it? As Jesus once warned:

"Judge not, lest you be judged yourself."

Now I know this is a big idea, a way of seeing life that is quite radical.

Please remember that I'm not saying, "Do not act," "Do not care," "Do not try and change what you feel inspired to change." I'm inviting you to explore a possibility, a choice in how you see your life and the world, one that involves the *foundation* to all speech and action.

At the very least this is an invitation to give yourself the very best platform of clarity, calm and positivity so that all your words and deeds aren't clouded and held back by stress, control, negativity. It means that you're not fighting battles you cannot win right now, so that you're not exhausting yourself over useless struggles.

This invitation is not to drop out but to drop what is holding you back. The invitation is, starting with your attitudes, judgements and beliefs, for you to actually become the greatest use to the world.

Okay?

The point remains:

What if? How will you know unless you do it?

Love

"*Don't change: Desire to change is the enemy of love.*
Don't change yourselves: Love yourselves as you are.
Don't change others: Love all others as they are.
Don't change the world: It is in God's hands and he knows.
And if you do that change will occur,
Marvellously in its own way and in its own time,
Yield to the current of life unencumbered by baggage."

- Anthony de Mello, Jesuit priest and spiritual teacher

In short, the amount of love you experience is directly related to the amount of acceptance, appreciation, and gratitude within you. Change doesn't need to be forced. If you want something different base it on an attitude of acceptance and appreciation first. Then things can happen fast.

However, in terms of acceptance and appreciation, have you ever noticed how harsh and critical your internal dialogue can be?

If you heard what you said to yourself being spoken out loud to another person, you would be shocked. But this inner dialogue has become so normal you don't notice it.

Don't think it has no effect. Not only does it affect how you feel and what you do and don't do, but your body responds to each and every thought you have. You can see this power of thought etched clearly in people's faces as you walk down the street.

This is important. Your relationship with yourself forms the basis to all your relationships.

Start actively noticing any harshness or criticism and flip it over. Acceptance and a positive attitude is the greatest foundation for any transformation. You want change? Start with acceptance and appreciation.

> *"To be beautiful means to be yourself. You don't need to be accepted by others. You need to accept yourself."*
>
> - Thich Nhat Hanh, Vietnamese Zen teacher

Love is inseparable from acceptance and appreciation, always.

You don't love yourself exactly as you are because there are parts of yourself that you judge as unacceptable. You resist who you are right now. Stop resisting, start accepting and you'll find nothing but love.

Unconditional love is unconditional appreciation which comes from unconditional acceptance. I love you exactly as you are.

It's just like that in romance. When you fall in love with someone, the love comes from you being in whole-hearted appreciation of them. But as time goes on you find things that are unacceptable. It feels like you fall out of love, but really you've fallen out of acceptance, you've fallen out of appreciation.

Love and Relationships

Here's the most amazing thing we do:

When we got together with our partners we were all over them. We did some serious work to make them notice. But it wasn't hard work, it was easy. We wanted to give.

Why?

You clearly liked what you saw and you saw what you liked. You wanted to see more, and more often – hence you were full on with appreciation and attention and giving to them.

This appreciation means attraction which turns to love; the relationship is fun, exciting, vibrant. Perhaps you even decide they're the one and you get married. End of story, happily ever after?

Not quite.

You see, you settle down. Since you have them, you start to cruise, you get lazy. You slowly stop working so hard to get and keep their attention, you stop being so active in your appreciation.

Being less active means you slip into taking them for granted.

Like many busy couples with their heads in busy to-do lists, your communication becomes based on the many jobs that need doing: "Go shopping," "Don't forget to pick up the kids," "What are we doing Tuesday night?" – your interaction becomes about doing stuff, and not about appreciating the relationship itself.

Continue down this road and you will probably start to notice what you don't like. The small things you ignored at first (or didn't even notice) get bigger; you start to nitpick.

Appreciation starts to shift to judgement as you focus more and more on what you wish you could change. Sometimes you do try to change them – with varying degrees of backlash. Perhaps your dynamic even shifts to one of condemnation.

The relationship gets stale, maybe argumentative, maybe one or both of you go elsewhere for a bit on the side that does give attention and appreciation. Maybe the relationship ends.

Where did the love go?

People change, people are incompatible, but ...

If you want to avoid the curse of so many stale relationships, if you want to be a part of a really loving, fun, supportive couple:

Keep doing the work.

If you do feel like your relationship is a little average, if it needs "something," all that's happened is that you stopped noticing and saying what you liked.

You were so busy and preoccupied with the little urgent things you started taking the other for granted. You stopped the gratitude, the appreciation, the small yet important things to say "I love you – I want you in my life." You might have been waiting to feel it before you said it. Or waiting to hear it first.

Relationships are living things, they need nurturing with your attention; prioritise what is truly important, be active. Have a solid foundation to your relationship by focusing overwhelmingly on what you like about the person.

Then you can, if needed, be honest. You can point out things that you would like the other to do or to change, and they'll take it well because the relationship has a solid base. They know you're on their side, that you've got their back.

Marriage counsellor and researcher Dr. John Gottman writes in his book, *What Predicts Divorce?*, that the ratio for a successful, thriving relationship is 5:1. This means five positive comments to every negative comment. Praise and gratitude far exceeds anything else.[7]

Now, there's no need to keep a tally and slack off when you have reached your quota for the day, what really works is having the attitude you're trying to win them, you're showing up with love and appreciation, every single day.

It'll make things so good for you, in every way, you won't want to stop. You get back what you give.

It'll also help you avoid the feelings trap.

The Feelings Trap

"What do you mean, 'feelings can be a trap'?" you may be thinking.

That's not what our culture teaches us, especially in relation to love. You know love because you *feel* it, right?

Feelings are an absolute trap.

Take, for example, wanting to get fit. Sometimes you feel like going to the gym, sometimes you don't. Whether you get to your goal depends on how much you're willing to just ignore your feelings and stick with your commitment to your goal.

We've talked a little about this, but do you see? Sometimes you feel really inspired and excited, sometimes you're not. Feelings come and go. Feelings are not a dependable source of information, really they aren't.

---

[7] This ratio also appears in successful teams of people. See the bibliography and notes section for more details.

You have a good night's sleep – you have one set of feelings. You have a bad night's sleep – you have another set. Just ask the parents of a new-born baby. Or ask someone with bipolar disorder about feelings.

Feelings are mercurial – fast-changing; and dependent on so much else.

You can't trust something that changes so much. You can't. That's why creating a foundation for your life by what you consistently focus on and what consistent actions you take is so important.

That's where commitment comes in and why it is so useful – as we were talking about earlier.

You listen less to what particular feeling you have, and just do what you said you would. Your life, your relationship, your fitness, your career: everything is created from the consistent choices you make day in, day out – and definitely not the feeling of the hour.

Expectations and Feelings in Love

Do you know what's even worse than a feeling?

An expectation.

An expectation that you should or should not be feeling something; hence the importance of innocence when it comes to feelings and relationships.

I've ruined so many great relationships simply because I wasn't "feeling" it. I wasn't feeling what I expected love should feel like.

So often I was looking for the feeling of excitement, that new, raw, "let's tear our clothes off right here in the kitchen" passion that's there at the beginning of each relationship.

When the excitement fades and a more subtle, perhaps mature, kind of love (with its associated feelings) comes in, I was left adrift: "I should be feeling 'a, b, c', and I'm not. She's obviously not the one. Let's look somewhere else for the excitement again."

Enter the hamster wheel of chasing the ever-elusive highs, only to find disappointment again and again and again.

So – be aware of your feelings of love or "not-love" and how you act on them. Don't wait to feel what you think you should be feeling.

The funny thing is if you have a solid giving attitude in your relationship, if you are trying to win them every day, you will definitely feel so much closeness and attraction. It may not be wild passion, but you're not in charge of that intensity of feeling.

What is for sure is that if you're focusing on what is wrong, even how the feelings are wrong, you're much more likely to feel apart, indifferent, negative, bored, even disgust with the other.

So much of your feelings depend on what you're focusing on.

The Grass Is Not Greener

> *"When the grass looks greener on the other side of the fence it's time to water your own lawn."*
>
> - Anon

Obviously, some of my relationships ended because we were unsuited, but so many ended because I didn't take responsibility for what I did – or didn't do – to bring my best to the relationship.

The common ingredient in all your relationships is you.

The grass is not greener on the other side of the fence. When you cross that fence, you'll still have the same head. You'll still have your tendency to judge, to compare, to take for granted, to not actively appreciate or give, to look at what else is on offer.

So, you're in a different relationship; but you have the same outlook, the same expectations and tendencies, the same mind that will never be satisfied. Your mind will never be content: and the more you search for something better, the more you will find.

You'll end up constantly looking for the next, better thing; and will never, ever be satisfied or content. No matter how good your relationship is now, your head will tell you otherwise, and you won't see it. You'll never make the most of what you have or really get to know the depths and the beauty of someone.

Especially for guys, the easy access to porn on the internet has amped up this tendency to constantly search. It's filled with – on a surface level – outrageously hot women who do everything and anything and there's no hard work involved (well, apart from the gymnastics).

All you have to do is turn up to the door with a pizza.

Needless to say, real relationships don't work like that. My dad told me that when he caught me with porn as a teenager – though I didn't understand at the time.

It took me a very long while to realise the damage porn was doing to the amount of love, satisfaction and contentment I was experiencing. It reinforced the tendency of my monkey mind to constantly look for the perfect banana (no pun intended), to disregard the happiness of what I had for the ever-present feeling there was something better.

Dreams are free – but sometimes you have to wake up to reality. If you want more from relationships and life, you need to see what you bring to the party, and it'll need to be more than just some fast food.

It's all About You

You can spend your life constantly seeking perfection; or you can create it now through what you focus on and what you do.

"Average Joe" relationships are all based on an attitude of "What can I *get* from this?" You'll find that the most amazing relationships are based on "How can I *give* to this? How can I make this better?"

What you bring to the table – your words and actions, your focus on making a relationship stronger and closer, your decision to make the choice to focus on what is good and right, your choice to make the most of what you have and rein in the tendency to look somewhere else for the next best thing – your choices are what brings your relationships truly Alive.

Don't wait to be given it. Don't wait to feel it. Start doing it.

If you want an amazing connection with someone, filled with love and excitement and understanding, support and adventures and discovery, deep contentment and satisfaction and fulfilment?

It's all about you.

Test It out for Yourself

The best thing about acceptance, appreciation, gratitude and love is that you can test it; you can try it out to see if it works for you.

Buddha said something that has stuck with me, along the lines of: Do not believe what I say. Do not make it an article of faith. Be willing – believe that it might be possible, but test it. Bite it, feel it out, try it. See if my words have truth in them for you.[8]

If it is true for one, it must be true for all. Otherwise it is not the truth.

So, test gratitude, try praise. Actively and consistently set out to appreciate people in your life. Be good to yourself, be aware of that harsh self-talk. Make lists of things that you are grateful about. Find the silver lining. In challenging situations or with challenging people, choose to appreciate something about it or them. Notice your judgement. Seek to build, not destroy. Don't get lazy. Notice when your focus goes to what is wrong or missing. Don't take. Give.

Keep it up and see what happens. How else are you going to know if it works or not?

---

[8] Because Buddha has been misquoted all over the shop, what he actually said, according to Buddhist texts, is as follows:

"Now, Kalamas, don't go by reports, by legends, by traditions, by scripture, by logical conjecture, by inference, by analogies, by agreement through pondering views, by probability, or by the thought, 'This contemplative is our teacher.' When you know for yourselves that, 'These qualities are skilful; these qualities are blameless; these qualities are praised by the wise; these qualities, when adopted and carried out, lead to welfare and to happiness' – then you should enter and remain in them."

But this makes my head hurt, and I prefer my version. You can quote me.

CHAPTER THIRTEEN

Choice 5: To Give
(when you want to get)

"If you knew what I know about the power of giving,
you would not let a single meal pass without sharing it in some way."

- Buddha

The Greatest Gift

We've been talking in depth about how some people choose to base their lives in terms of what they believe to be good, enjoyable, beautiful and righteous. Others choose to see life in terms of what they believe is wrong, what is missing or lacking; what they don't have.

It's a simple choice of perspective, but it dramatically affects how you live. Some find that they have everything to give and share; others believe they have everything to get and protect.

What makes both appreciation and gratitude so powerful, especially when they are expressed outwardly, is that they are acts of giving. What brings any relationship alive is giving. What makes a life become a Life is giving.

Chances are if you give a lot, you live in a world that is abundant and full, peaceful and beautiful. If you give little, it's likely that the world you live in is the opposite.

Giving is the key that unlocks more. More joy, beauty, abundance, grace. It is the single greatest thing you can do to experience less fear, less judgement and more wholeness. Giving transforms your inner state, your outer appreciation of life, and literally, your whole world.

Give of Yourself

> *"You give but little when you give of your possessions.*
> *It is when you give of yourself that you truly give."*

— Kahlil Gibran, author of *The Prophet*

To really experience the power of giving you're just going to have to do it. If you're interested in living a life of 200%, find as many ways as you can to give to someone else.

It could be actively being appreciative or grateful; it could be helping in some way, small or large, known or unknown — a smile, a supportive word, a helping hand, a donation of time, expertise or money — whatever it is, just get started with an attitude of giving and of service.

When you do, you immediately experience the rewards of giving. You give not so much because it benefits another, but because it directly benefits you.

Even, and particularly, if you are feeling low, depressed, or deprived — perhaps you are worried about not having enough money or that your life isn't working out the way you want it to – get up out of your funk and find a way to help someone else. It will transform your mood. Consistently done, it changes your whole outlook on life.

Here's the secret to giving:

When you give, you begin to realise how much you have. Your attention goes there and away from what you don't have. You realise that you don't have to hold on so tight. It makes you realise how abundant you are, how lack was an idea.

Giving keeps you humble; it makes you grateful and it enlivens your life. Happy people are those who have found a way to give.

That's the secret of giving – it enhances *your* life.

> *"Wise are those who give. Wiser still are those*
> *who look for opportunities to give."*
>
> - Maharishi Sadashiva Isham, Ishaya teacher

Many people are willing to give, when asked. Not many are so aware of the power of going out of their way to find ways to give.

The more you give, the closer you come to live from the source of happiness and love itself. The more you give, the more you realise you have nothing to fear; that you never needed to try to protect or secure what is important to you, in fact you couldn't. The more you give, the more you realise that what is truly important only increases by being given.

The more you give, the more you realise your own innate freedom. Not because you deserve to be free, but because you were born free, and simply believed differently.

Giving is the very essence of life itself.

Be the Change

> *"Be the change you wish to see in the world."*
>
> - Mahatma Gandhi, Indian political and spiritual leader

It is a fascinating and inviolable certainty of life: what you give tends to be what you get.

If you are smart – and you are smart, otherwise you wouldn't be reading this – you may come to the following conclusion:

If you get what you give, it would be a good idea to give what you want to receive.

It works at the most basic level: if you want more hugs, give more hugs. If you want more friends, give more friendship. If you want happier people around you, be more happy. If you want more love, give more love.

But it even works at a more subtle and abstract level: if you want more understanding, give more understanding. If you want more honesty, be more honest. More clarity? Be clearer. More patience and tolerance and mutual respect? Be all of that.

> *"For it is in giving that we receive."*
>
> - St. Francis of Assisi, Italian Catholic friar

The more you give, the more you get. It's the simplest, yet most misunderstood rule there is. Everything starts with you. You can sit at home waiting, needing, or you can get out and give. Ironically then you start receiving, more than you can ever imagine.

It's the coolest thing once you see it:

Loving, open, happy people have a whole world that is loving and open and happy. They attract very similar people.

Scared and anxious people tend to create events and people that make them scared and anxious, giving them more reason to be scared and anxious.

If you find yourself pointing the finger at people and insisting that they are more x, y or z for whatever reason, it's an excellent sign you need to look at yourself.

Be the change you wish to see in the world.

That single act, bringing the focus of change to within yourself, changes more than you can possibly imagine.

Everything starts with you.

And I'm not saying to ignore behaviour that is unacceptable, but I think one of the best guides to making choices in relation to others is from Jesus:

"Do to others as you would have them do to you."

Treat others how you wish to be treated yourself. Give the person exactly what you would want if you were in their place.

Imagine a world where everyone did that. Where everyone gave to others exactly what we ourselves want from life ...

That is the revolution the world needs right there.

It springs not from our political, religious, sporting, entertainment leaders but from your own heart, right now. Nothing more, nothing less.

But don't take my word for it; do it yourself. Even if you disagree, try it. Prove me (and Gandhi) right or wrong by putting your money where your mouth is.

Save the world starting with yourself. You are the one person you can change – so you might as well get going.

One more thing.

Ever tried to actually change someone? In fact, do you realise you try and change all your loved ones?

Stop. It's futile. People dig their heels in deep when they feel someone is trying to change them. But they do respond to a) openness and b) change in others. It all points back to you.

Give Wholeness

> *"Treat people as if they are what they could be,*
> *and they will become what they are capable of being."*
>
> -Johann Wolfgang von Goethe, German author

The greatest gift you can give someone is to see them as whole.

You can't be much help if you see them as being broken or lacking – and yet that is a common way of helping others: the "poor you" approach.

Much better to see what is right about a person, and make that the foundation of all your giving. See a person as capable, resourceful and whole, rather than seeing what they don't have, or what you think they need.

When you look at a person in terms of lack, you don't see the person, you just see the need or the problem.

The greatest thing you can give to anyone is to choose to give them wholeness; see them in perfection and they will respond to your gift.

Appreciation and gratitude is unconditional. It admits no lack or need. In telling someone, "I really like ..." there are no ifs and buts or shoulds. There is wholeness in even the smallest compliment.

What you will find is that all giving becomes a conversation. Not "I help you," but "We give to each other." You become open to receiving, to truly connecting with another.

The fullness of giving begins with the fullness of vision.

True Compassion

Giving isn't feeling someone's pain as if it was your own. There is no need to get down in the pit with someone; suffering shared is only suffering doubled – yet that's what many people do.

Sometimes when you can't do anything else, this "poor you" approach feels like you are helping. But what tends to happen is you reinforce the suffering of their situation, the helplessness, not the choices that they have despite their circumstances.

The "poor you" approach reinforces someone's status as a victim. It reinforces blame and powerlessness. It helps the person to abandon all personal responsibility for where they are and what they can do next.

Seeing someone as whole, as not broken or lacking is a means of helping them help themselves in the greatest possible sense.

This in no way means you don't care – but it's holding a bigger picture of caring.

There's an old adage that sums up true compassion perfectly:

> *"You can give someone a fish and feed them for a day,*
> *or you can teach someone how to fish and feed them for a lifetime."*

I'd add to that:

> *"If you teach them how to teach, you feed a village forever."*

People need different things at different times.

Sometimes it is a short-term boost – it is giving them a fish, a handout, a hug, a listening ear, some comfort. Sometimes it's more long term – it's advice or education, it's making them aware of their choices, it may be honesty.

You won't know unless you are present and tune into what they need, perhaps even asking them what they need. It is having the wisdom to see this, all based on your vision that even though they may be in need, they aren't a victim, they aren't lacking.

Whatever you actually do or say, compassion is a ladder up and out of suffering. It is a means not of reinforcing their situation but helping them out of it – if they choose to use that means of getting themselves out.

Unconditionally giving – without regard for whether help is accepted or not – is always the bottom line, and is the most difficult part of giving. Because it is so easy for you to become invested and attached to the person "getting" it – to them listening and changing because of your "wise" words and actions.

Allowing someone their own path is true giving, because at some point they'll learn, and truly learn, from personal experience. At some point they'll start to take responsibility for their choices – but you can't force that on anyone. You can't make them see that, ever.

The best thing you can do to help is to actually be fully responsible for your own peace and happiness. It is the very thing you throw away if you get upset because you've tried to help someone and they've ignored you. All giving is based on you stepping up into your choice to live 200%.

Giving Unconditionally

In the past I would read in spiritual books about unconditional giving and how the most powerful giving is done without concern or regard for the result, without interest for "getting" anything. This threw me, because I saw how I always gave conditionally, to get something in return.

When I read these books, I couldn't understand how someone could actually give unconditionally. It made me see how everything I did for someone else was for something; so they would give back to me, so they would think I was a good person.

I saw how I'd give to a girl so she'd think I was nice and might sleep with me. When I became more "spiritual" I gave to get good karma, or to atone for past regrets, or whatever. Rarely did I freely give for giving's sake. Seeing my relationships like this really gave me an excellent insight into my own mind ... but giving unconditionally seemed *impossible*.

Now, of course you get when you give, like I was saying above. Giving sets up a speedy return system – to you. But it's true: when you master giving you stop being concerned with, or attached to, what comes back. Giving – and receiving – becomes a cycle as natural as breathing is likely to be to you at the moment:

The breath goes out; the natural and automatic response is that the breath comes in. You do very little. It goes out freely, it comes back in freely, and so the natural cycle continues. You give freely, it comes back in the most unexpected ways – but it always comes back in.

Understanding that I profited from giving in all the myriad ways we've been talking about helped me to start giving more. It gave me the courage to give in areas of my life I was most scared of. It helped me test the waters and after that, practise becoming better at giving without conditions.

What we're talking about in this whole book is practising and learning some new choices, some new skills, so they become habitual, natural.

Just because perfecting a particular skill seems so far away from you right now, it's no reason to disregard it. In fact, it's all the more reason to work at it. You want to: there are huge rewards from getting even a little bit better at giving unconditionally.

By practising giving it will show you exactly when your overwhelming concern is about what you can get from the situation, or when you are attached to a certain outcome. This is just another form of control or manipulation and an attempt to secure happiness in outside circumstances or from a person. In learning to give unconditionally, you're learning to become free from all such conditions, you're learning to be free in every part of your life.

So, whether you feel like you can give unconditionally or not, just do it. Begin giving anyway. It will show you so much about yourself. It will show you how you can be free of any conditions and limits on your own happiness and freedom. It will show you that you can be free from fear.

You'll know you're giving unconditionally when you're innocently living your life, and people thank you for it.

Giving To Yourself

Sometimes a "no" is the best thing you can give. Some, such as many mothers, give too much. They give and they give until they are empty and everyone around them is dependent. Then guilt comes whenever they want to do something for themselves – even popping out to the shops causes a major internal upheaval.

Giving to yourself is equally important as giving to others – in fact, it is most important. You cannot give to anyone if you are drained. Giving to yourself is never selfish. When you're at 100% everyone wins. When you're grumpy, resentful, guilty? No one wins, least of all yourself.

Safety briefings on aeroplanes tell you this too – put on your own oxygen mask first, then help others. Makes sense doesn't it?

A common reason for giving is to get love or self-worth. If you realise you're doing this? You most definitely need to cut those chains of dependence that you have created. Find a source of that sustenance within you so you can give freely and unconditionally.

Love Is Not Something You Need

All over the world there are people needing love. The central drama of all existence is "He/she doesn't love me!" It's the central preoccupation of humanity; people looking for love, in particular, looking to be loved.

My experience with relationships was no different. They were all about me getting love. Underlying this was the fear that I needed to protect my heart from being broken. If I gave anything, it was with concern about what I would receive. I gave love, and if (and only if) I got more, I gave more.

I exaggerate a little, but it was like a financial transaction. I was a cautious investor in love, dipping my toe, constantly looking for the return, protecting my "savings."

There is zero freedom in giving only when you get. There is also very little return.

The truth is most relationships in the world are founded on "What can I *get* from this person?" The best relationships are the opposite. If you make everything about "How can I give?" you will have not only the greatest relationship, but also the most rich and magical of lives.

Why?

Because love is not something you need; it is something you are. There is no shortage of love, it increases by being given away. If you want more love in your life, give more love. Just give and you will see you never actually needed anything. You will see your heart can never be broken.

When you fully and completely realise that love is not gotten but given, no longer will you insist that someone loves you. You are free to love freely, unconditionally, without fear or needing to protect. You can live life without restriction – with open arms and an open, innocent heart, and life is a zillion times better.

Money, Scarcity and Abundance

> *"Money is like love; it kills slowly and painfully the one who withholds it, and enlivens the other who turns it on his fellow man."*
>
> - Kahlil Gibran, author and poet

I used to confuse money with happiness. I thought if I had more money I would be more happy, more free. But what I actually wanted was just to be free. Money is a powerful indicator that showed me, and anyone actually, exactly where they are not free but bound and limited.

You see, I never enjoyed spending money. I hated seeing money go out. I had more than enough, but I would wake in the morning with all my thoughts being money worries. I was constantly anxious around money.

Giving evaporated that.

The reason people don't give much is because they give power to scarcity: "I would give, but I don't have enough. I need to protect my interests."

That belief, "I don't have enough," is like a monster under the bed. Scarcity gets bigger the more you believe in it; your focus makes it grow.

At what point *will* you have enough? How much money *is* enough?

Be aware that abundance – the feeling of having more than enough to give away – is a *feeling*: it has no relation whatsoever to the number in your bank account, and yet it will shape your behaviour. You have enough or don't have enough, you give or you hold tightly, and are constantly anxious of where your next money will come from, all based not on reality but a feeling, a belief.

Scarcity is a powerful belief – it gets wrapped up around your feelings of survival itself. But if you want to change that? If you're tired of waking in the morning and your first thought being about money?

It is this limiting belief of not enough that you're giving away when you make a commitment to live a life based in giving.

By deciding to give more in being more generous to my friends and loved ones, I started to enjoy what money could give and what giving gave me. In no way was I irresponsible, but by being very alert to feelings of lack and constriction around money and acting differently, my world started to change.

Quietly, the more I gave, the more I got. The more I gave, the more my fear around lack of money lessened, until it vanished. I can't tell you how good it feels not to worry about money.

I noticed the flow of money much more. Before it was always a focus on money going out. The more I loosened my grip, the more I noticed money coming in as well. I enjoyed an increasing gratitude for both spending *and* receiving. My world became not based on lack, but on abundance.

Money is no different to love or anything else. The tighter you hold on, the less you can receive. The more you open to possibility, the more personal and transformational gifts money can give you.

Many spiritual traditions realise the power of giving, especially money, suggesting you might tithe. Tithing is the practice of giving away a percentage of your income, traditionally 10%. If you wish to do something similar, it will truly illuminate your beliefs around money.

Explore what your mind says when you tithe. It will hate it every now and then, but give anyway. Increasingly the sheer joy of financially supporting something you appreciate becomes more dominant, and your relationship with money, scarcity and abundance will change forever.

The Gift

The gift of giving is that it sets you free.

Giving shows you what, in this entire universe, is truly valuable. Giving shows you that you have more than enough. It shows you the power of your attention. It shows you that you create the reality of your life by your choices.

If you want to know what the end of fighting and struggling feels like; give.

If you want to know the end of fear and emptiness; give.

If you want to know the end of needing and victimhood; give.

If you want to know a world of fullness, of love and peace; give.

If you want to be free; give.

If you want more in your life, just give. Let giving be the teacher. Just start and see what it shows you about yourself and your assumptions about the world. Keep looking for places to give and you'll find the world is a bounty of riches; you'll realise your true nature is nothing but joyful, constant giving.

You create your reality. Every choice you make shapes it. Make life how you want it to be.

CHAPTER FOURTEEN

Choice 6: To Be Here Now
(when you want to be somewhere else)

"Many people are alive but don't touch the miracle of being alive."

- Thich Nhat Hanh, Vietnamese Zen teacher

Be Alive, Be Present

Being present is the single greatest thing you can do for your life.

Being present means you can be focused, clear, creative, and happy too.

Being present means you can give 100% to whatever you do. Every part of your life benefits when you are present to it.

Being present means you manage – and can ultimately end – all stress, anxiety, overwhelm, judgement, anger ... all negativity.

Being present means you can be calm and content, no matter the circumstances. When other people are losing it, you keep it.

Being present means you can be free from reactive patterns and flying off the handle. It means you have choice, very real choice, in what you do and how you live your life.

Being present means life becomes enjoyable and easy. Life makes sense when you are here and alive to it. Life takes on a deeper purpose when you show up for it.

Being present means you show up to what is real. Right here, right now. Not a memory, not a wish or a fear but reality, this.

Being present is so simple. There is nothing simpler. Just wake up. Be alive, be here, be in the same place as your body.

Stop sleep-walking through your life – be present, be alive.

Don't Let Life Slip by

"Life is what happens while you are busy making other plans."

- John Lennon, musician

It's a funny old thing, life. It's happening here, now and most people aren't aware of it. They miss out on life itself, thinking and planning about some other moment, some moment in which they believe life will happen.

So many people believe that some other moment will be better or is more important than this one. Now becomes ignored as a transition to a more ideal future, like a bus journey to be endured until you finally get "there." Each day is filled with planning and looking forward to this other "better" moment, while now – which is actually the whole of life – slips by.

"Most people treat the present moment as if it were an obstacle that they need to overcome. Since the present moment is life itself, it is an insane way to live."

- Eckhart Tolle, spiritual teacher

Do you do that? Is your life going on right under your nose while you are elsewhere? Are you living in an insane way?

Unless you are present and alive to life, to this moment, you are missing out. And no one has an infinite amount of time to get to the task of really, truly living. It's something you need to get onto very, very soon.

I want to ask you:

What will it take to wake you up?

What will wake you up to the fact that the way you're living your life means it's ending, one moment at a time? While you ... you are somewhere else, lost in your head, thinking and planning and predicting and regretting and reacting?

When are you going to stop wasting life, being lost in the past or the future, wishing, dreaming that you were anywhere but here?

When are you going to make the most of each and every moment?

When are you going to start living life so that it begins afresh, now?

Are you going to wait until you're on your death-bed? Looking back and realising that you have no more time left, that you can't postpone any longer?

Wake up to your own life; take it and go.

Live your life fully. It requires so little, just your attention applied now. Such a small, simple sacrifice – an act of giving – and you get so much.

If you don't, who will? If not now, when?

Where Are You?

The greatest way to live the best of lives is to spend as much time as you can in the same place as your body.

That may sound funny, but humans are the best time travellers. We are anywhere but here in this moment; we are always in the past or future. We live everywhere but in our bodies, and we spend an awesome amount of time in our heads.

You will find you become so much more efficient and, perhaps more importantly, enjoy yourself so much more when you are alive solely to this moment.

Being fully in your body is the reason you enjoy what you enjoy so much, whether it is golf or knitting, climbing rocks or making music, exercising or just sitting, watching.

When you do these things you become very present. You get out of your head; your senses broaden; you become aware.

You become absorbed in the task and in this moment. It captivates you, invigorates you. You become Alive. You get into the "Zone." The noise of the mind is transcended for an experience of inner stillness; it all becomes quiet, silent, full, simple.

But this experience isn't about what you are doing or where you are. Not at all.

I always thought that kayaking brought me so much joy because it was out in nature; because it was adventurous, exciting and physically challenging.

It is all these things, but critically the experience of being in the Zone came not because I was up a river, but because being up a river meant I let go of thinking so much and focused on the here and now.

Kayaking was a distraction from my mind; it meant I let go of the story of my life. My life was somewhere else, but now was now. Kayaking was "me" time! The added challenge meant I had to fully focus on this moment – my concern about my bills or the argument with my girlfriend could have no relevance; otherwise, my friends or I would get hurt.

Interesting isn't it?

Your love for what you do stems in a large part because it gives you the experience of being completely present and alive, absorbed and immersed in the task and the moment. It is about tapping into inner stillness, in the midst of activity, that brings you happiness and satisfaction.

A recent study showed this: a group of subjects were studied closely and were found to spend 47% of their day, on average, mind-wandering. This means nearly *half* of most people's days are spent staring out the mental – or actual – window. Half of a person's life is spent in a dream.

When asked how satisfied or content the subjects were, it was found that happiness had *nothing* to do with the task the subjects were involved in. You would think that an interesting or absorbing task would lead to increased happiness. But, no, in reality, satisfaction wasn't related to the task. It was related to how focused and present the subject was.

If you want to be more satisfied, content, happy? If you want to be in a state of Flow? Get more present.

As I have learned to become more present, I've discovered that I can have the same fullness, absorption and satisfaction from, say, washing the dishes as from being out on the river.

Being in the outdoors may give me the additional blast I get from doing what I love, but the sense of being alive and absorbed, completely and utterly present to this moment? That is now available in any moment I choose – no matter what I do.

Even if you live an incredibly busy life, you can only do one thing at a time – so do that one thing.

Be totally absorbed in it, in this moment. Don't half-arse do it while thinking about what you want to do next. Don't be somewhere else.

Be here, fully and completely, in the same place as your body. It is the only way to live an Alive life.

Just Pretend That This Moment Is the Only Moment That Exists

A friend of mine – a Bright Path Ishaya teacher of meditation – loves to tell his students to pretend that this moment is the only moment that exists.

What he's getting them to explore is what happens when they assume that there is no other moment in time – only now.

How about that? What happens when you do this? When you just assume now is all you have – when you let go and get present to this, to what is here, to what is now? What do you experience when you do this?

It means you only have to deal with right now. It means you're suspending control of everything else, everything that isn't here. What a relief!

If you're like most people, you'll spend a lot of time every day reliving the past, soaking in past glories or regrets, or anticipating the future, dreaming of a better moment to come, worrying about things that haven't happened yet, or trying to control or predict the future.

Reliving past memories or dreaming about the future can be pleasant, sometimes, for sure, but past/future thinking is also the source of all anxiety and worry, all resentment, guilt, regret, frustration. Being in the past or the future is the cause of *all* your stress and struggle.

If you pretend that now is the only moment that exists and get present – if you tune into this moment – you relax and let go. You can't be present and go over what happened or what could happen; it's impossible. A space opens up in you, around you – something you probably didn't notice before.

When you get out of your thoughts, you will find that all is well. Nothing can be wrong when you let go of everything else and give your full attention to this moment.

Life gets extraordinarily simple and easy when you take it one moment at a time. Just now. And now. And now – meeting the need of the moment, free of the burden of the past and the future.

Here you are. Really be here. Don't worry about anything else.

Really, honestly, if I could give you one thing, it would be to realise that a peaceful, happy, enjoyable and efficient life is right here.

As the spiritual teacher Eckhart Tolle so beautifully puts it,

> *"If you get the inside right, the outside will fall into place. As soon*
> *as you honor the present moment, unhappiness and struggle*
> *dissolve, and life begins to flow with joy and ease ... whatever you*
> *do becomes imbued with a sense of quality, care, and love*
> *– even the most simple action."*

Bring yourself back when you forget and you will find it easier and easier to stay here now.

A Present Life, Free From Suffering

There are zero problems here, now, in this moment. Honestly. All your suffering vanishes – *all* of it – when you fully immerse yourself in the presence of now.

This is a huge idea, a bold idea – and your mind may hate it – but it doesn't make it un-true.

Let's investigate: assume this moment is the only moment there is. Get super present, be aware of now. Be innocent and fresh. Drop all expectations, insistences, resistances and just meet this moment face to face, as it is. Truly tune in, give your whole being to this moment in time.

What else does your experience of now need?

Nothing. It is full, rich, complete. Now requires nothing, there is nothing wrong ... when you are *fully* here.

Your mind may still rebel.

It may try to negate your experience of now, saying "Yes, but ...", as in "Yes, but ... yesterday I was so full of fear/anger/sadness," or "Yes, but ... my daughter is very sick in hospital right now and I'm so anxious about her," or "Yes, but ... tomorrow I have to have a really tough conversation with my boss and I'm worried about it."

One of the mind's greatest tricks is convincing you that the causes of fear and worry and suffering are present, they are very real now. However, your mind is anywhere but here. It is constantly trying to drag you off into some other place and time, and suffering only becomes real when you follow it.

Suffering – overload, overwhelm, reacting blindly – doesn't happen when you're fully present.

Your mind will tell you that you're irresponsible and uncaring if you let go of the events and the challenges of all other places and times to experience the one place your life is, the one place you can do anything about – here and now.

Don't let your mind convince you.

How useful is it when you are worried or stressed about something you can do nothing about? How caring is it when you're so consumed in a past or upcoming event you can't be present with the people in front of you? How useful is suffering to you, or indeed anyone else?

It's not.

A skilful, joyful, compassionate and suffering-free life is being able to let go of all other places and moments so you can give yourself fully to what is happening right in front of you. Here is where life is!

Again, don't get me wrong – in being present I'm not saying ignore your challenges and what you have to do, not at all.

I'm saying truly see what problems are actually here, now, right in front of you. See how your mind wants to remove you from this moment to go over a situation that isn't here. See all this mind stuff and ignore it, instead take a half-step back and be present; be fully alive.

How Will I Plan?

Here comes the most common "Yes, but ..." objection: "Yes, but how will I plan my life?"

You still plan for the future – and learn from the past – it's just that you are able to maintain that "half-step back" from all the processing and planning and mental and emotional churning.

This half-step back means you stay calm and clear, aware and present. You still think and do and get going, but you don't get lost in it. When you're done planning, you put it down and move to the next thing. Clean and clear. Present, focused, active perhaps – but relaxed.

In terms of sketching out a future: you focus on this moment in time as you create a plan, book the tickets, pack your bags. All is as before – but with the critical distinction that you are minus distraction and worry and self-doubt and "what if's" and all that useless mind-wandering and interference that typically goes with any plan. And then, once you've made the plan, you let it go. It's done – you're present and onto to the next thing.

196

It is the exact difference between your mind using you and you using your mind.

Your mind is an excellent tool – but if you're like most people it's a tool you've lost control of.

The problem isn't so much thinking, but not being able to stop thinking.

The problem of humanity is that we can't put a particular thought pattern "down." We can't let go and focus on what we want to focus on. We get lost and caught up in so much thinking, unable to distance ourselves from a busy, worried, regretful, negative, angry, frustrated mind. It can be incredibly harsh. As entrepreneur and Nobel Peace Prize nominee Bryant McGill notes:

"The worst bullies you will ever encounter in your life
are your own thoughts."

And you might not even be aware quite how much it's happening – all of this seems "normal."

Getting present doesn't stop you living; on the contrary, getting present allows you to live.

It enables you to leave behind all the mind stuff that means you can't choose for calm, focus or happiness in any moment you like. It means you drop all the mind stuff that causes suffering, that limits you, that prevents you from living the life you want.

Being present means you realise what you are in control of, and what you're not. It makes you realise when you're resisting an undeniable reality, or when you can move forward and make a change.

You realise how useless, in fact, how absolutely weakening and destructive some thought patterns are, and that you are able to ignore them at will.

You become firmly based in this moment in time, not as a transition to a better moment, but living in the one place your body is, right here, right now. This is it.

So, assume away! Assume that this moment is all you have. You can – and should – plan for a future, but realise that now is the only place you can live and be Alive.

Do You Know Why You Don't Spend Much Time in This Moment?

Have you ever felt like you are wrestling with a constantly active mind? One that you just can't shut up? One that can't stop thinking in ways you don't want to think, or one you can't prevent from reliving past moments you want to forget? One that tears you out of now, no matter how good your intentions are to stay here?

Do you feel like you have been given to your mind, as opposed to your mind being given to you?

Of course you do, you're human.

Struggling against our own minds is the biggest problem humanity has. If you ask anyone with some self-awareness about this, it's likely they would say they would like to be able to remove a large portion of their minds. I saw a recent study that showed a significant number of people would rather self-harm by giving themselves painful electric shocks than sit alone with their thoughts.

Your mind never rests. It is never content; it can be very abusive. It is always active – that's what it does. You find a bit of happiness and calm, and then your mind is gone, searching for the next thing. Your mind can never be content because it's always on the hunt, always going.

If you keep it fuelled by your unconscious yet active attention, your mind will do nothing else but look out for sources of trouble and anguish. It will remind you of all your mistakes and reinforce all your short-comings. It will jump from one anxiety or guilt or worry to another, one reactive trigger to another, one hope to another. No wonder it's hard to find lasting presence, happiness or peace.

The problem with over-thinking is that, through habit, we have let the mind become the boss.

You've let the mind into the driving seat and it's gotten away, going for it, predicting, guessing, checking, worrying, doubting, comparing, the whole works.

In no way is this relaxing. It's inefficient too. Because the mind is never present, you rarely can focus on, or meet, the true need of this moment. You rarely show up for life.

For the fullest, richest life possible, you have to learn to be the boss of your mind. Being the boss doesn't mean closing it down or shutting it up. It means realising what the mind is – and having a different, bigger perspective.

You Are NOT What You Think You Are

You think you are the contents of your mind, but actually you are much bigger than that.

You are awareness.

You are unbounded, rich, full, still awareness, unlimited, humming with potential. Yet, you – through habit and not knowing any alternative – become what your awareness gets latched onto.

If you have a happy thought, and believe it, you become happy. If you have an anxious thought, and believe it, you become anxious. If you have the thought "I can't do it" and believe it, guess what? You can't do it. If you have the thought "I am fat" and believe it, you'll experience yourself that way no matter how false and unhelpful it is. Focus on any thought long enough and you are likely to become a believer. Focusing on the thought "I am Jesus Christ" long enough won't make you that, but it may just give you a messiah complex.

For the longest time all you have noticed is the same old loops of thought that are floating around inside your skull. You're so involved in the detail you don't see anything else. You notice the content but rarely the context. The words but not the page. It's like noticing fish swimming but not seeing the water.

The world is a huge and wondrous place, but if you're focused on thoughts you just won't notice much of it. All you'll notice is the thoughts.

The trouble is you're so close, so lost in them you don't clearly see them, you're not fully aware of what they're telling you. You believe you are your thoughts; you become what they say.

They shape and filter everything. They are the lens that colours what you perceive. They are the beliefs that dictate who you are and who you aren't; what you notice and how you notice it.

The Jesuit priest and spiritual teacher Anthony de Mello once wrote:

*"Thought can organize the world so well that you
are no longer able to see it."*

Similarly, Buddha reportedly said:

*"We are what we think. All that we are arises with our thoughts.
With our thoughts, we make the world."*

Change your mind, change your world – perhaps I have said that before?

Step back from your mind and something special happens. You start to see clearly, innocently, calmly, with total awareness. You can have a direct experience of the field of awareness beyond your thoughts. You can experience the context – what is real and doesn't change, exactly as it is – and all without a fight, without effort at all.

Being the boss of your mind begins right here – it's as simple as being who you really are.

Stepping Beyond

For you to gain lasting peace and happiness with effortless focus, you honestly don't need to spend precious time and energy struggling with your mind. You don't need to force the mind to be quiet. You don't need to change it, at all.

All that is involved is relaxing, taking a half-step back, and detaching from the rollercoaster of thought. It certainly helps to find some good tools like meditation to enable you to do this, if you haven't already.

When you stop focusing on thoughts and become present and aware, even just for a moment, this quiet – but hugely significant – change I mention above comes in.

The half-step back means there is a sense of calm, of space. You notice the bigger picture; the mind becomes smaller, quieter in comparison.

You start to realise you *have* a mind, you *have* thoughts – just like an ocean has fish – but you are not them. Just as the ocean has no reason to fight the fish, you have no reason to fight the mind. Stop focusing on thoughts and you start to be free of struggle; you start to become independent of the mind.

You become content, satisfied. This source of contentment wasn't ever far away; it's just that you have been distracted, listening to your mind trying to be helpful by telling you about anything and everything.

You also become ready. Gently focused. Alert. Ready for anything, all possibilities.

You can meet the need of this moment because you're not absorbed in the mind talk about the last moment or the next one. You can direct your considerable attention to anything you wish, not just what your mind tells you is important.

If you become the boss of your mind, you are free.

Free to put your attention on anything you wish. Free to choose. Free to follow what is most important to you, your highest desire. Free to finally show up for life, to participate fully in it.

Most importantly, you are free to realise who you really are.

Know Thyself

Are you aware that you have voices in your head, that you talk to, all the time? If you, on reading that sentence, thought "What a load of rubbish, I don't have any voices, I don't talk to myself" – that's exactly what I'm talking about.

Talking to yourself is nothing to be ashamed of; the fact is everyone does it all the time. You have a team of consultants and coaches and advisers in your head – the whole spectrum: cheerleaders and naysayers, geniuses and village idiots.

However, if you want peace of mind, freedom from stress, and 200% of life, you'll need to be aware that this voice in your head is merely that: a voice, something passing through, not necessarily *true*.

When you aren't aware, you have no choice. You follow and do and feel and react according to whatever voice is there in the moment. You've lived so close to the voice in your head for so long it seems like there is no option – you automatically follow what it says.

It's one result when you go with the voice that says "I'm hungry," completely another path when you believe the voice that states "I can't" or "I'm stupid." Perhaps even more insidious is the voice that commands "I should."

In awareness you have choice.

When you are aware of the voice in your head, life stops being a series of reactive "what you have always done" habits and starts being based on creative choices – you start consciously living your life. You become aware of restrictive or limiting patterns and habits and can make other decisions.

Choice is the key word, always. Choice does not require effort. It doesn't require your mind to shut up or go away, it really doesn't; all it takes is noticing what is there and shifting your attention to something else.

Try This

Take a moment, and even just for a couple of minutes, stop and observe your thoughts.

Watch. Notice them. Let them come and let them go. To begin, try counting them. Assign each one a number as simply as if you were counting clouds in the sky as they pass by.

Don't count the counter – you'll get confused.

For each thought there doesn't have to be a reaction. Every thought can just be a number. Every thought can just arise and then fall away to wherever it came from.

Equally, just because you think it, it doesn't mean it is true. A thought can simply be an idea, a label, an interpretation or an option. A thought can simply be a passing energy. Does that make sense?

For example, there doesn't need to be a link between a "bad" thought and feeling bad – you don't have to choose the option of feeling bad, you could choose to just observe and let go.

Just because you have thoughts it doesn't mean that you are the thoughts. Because you can be aware of the contents of your mind, it means you must be more than those contents. Your thoughts need not define or be the limit of you.

If this is so, if you aren't your mind, if you aren't your beliefs, if you have choice, then what are you? What else is there when you take that half-step back in awareness?

Be aware and find out. Know thyself.

It's worth doing. To me, two of the most important questions for anyone are always "Who are you?" and "How do you want to live?"

Whatever the answer is for you, don't live blindly. There is always more beyond the voices. There is always choice. Always.

The Practice of Being Here, Now – Always

"The aim of life is to live, and to live means to be aware,
joyously, drunkenly, serenely, divinely aware."

- Henry Miller, author

You want to be able to choose to be present any time you wish?

You want to be able to effortlessly focus and transcend doubt and fear? You want to be able to ignore anxiety and worry? You want to be able to create new programmes in your mind that don't trigger you into guilt or frustration or rage?

You want to rest and recharge, to recuperate quickly, to enjoy better, deeper sleep?

You want more enjoyment? You want to be able to choose to have calm, focus, happiness and peace in any moment you wish?

You want to discover that still, silent, fully present space that is free from all the ups and downs of the mind and the emotions?

You need to learn to meditate; it is essential to free choice. It is the key tool that will give you greater awareness.

There is so much guff, so much misunderstanding around what meditation is. It stops a huge number of people taking up something that could seriously save lives.

Meditation gives you the ability to be free; to not get stuck in your thoughts or feelings. It gives the ability to maintain that half-step back from all the voices in your head. It is at the heart of living 200%.

Through meditation you develop the ability to purely witness, to allow thoughts and emotions to come and go. Meditation gives you perspective and clarity; the ability to stay afloat and not drown in negative, overwhelming or harmful mind stuff.

You develop the ability to choose what you focus on.

You gain the ability to enjoy every – *every* – single aspect of your life.

You get the ability to be completely present and alive to now; detaching completely from a past and a future you have no control over.

Perhaps there is a negative thought or a worry or a doubt. Meditation isn't about banishing it; it is about simply letting it be there but not getting wrapped up in it.

It is there, but it isn't you. You don't get lost in it any more. Or if you do, you can choose to let go immediately, simply, effortlessly.

Meditation in action is when you take this ability to not react into your everyday life.

Say something doesn't go the way you want it to. You are able to be unaffected, to remain calm and clear and see what you can do about the situation – if anything.

You don't get wrapped up in drama any more. Being calm and at peace is so much more enjoyable, and you know how to choose for it. Drama becomes so pointless.

You break the chains of reaction – when someone says or does something, no longer are you pulled to and fro like a monkey on a chain.

You give up your ticket to the rollercoaster – life becomes one super stable, super enjoyable, super effective moment. Joy and contentment are your overwhelming responses to life.

This is good. That is good too. Everything is good.

From that calmness and clarity comes the ability to live the very best, truest version of yourself. And all it takes is a little practice. A little commitment to being that greatest version of you.

You can do this: it is who you have been all along.

So stop. Take a moment from trying to work stuff out or trying to control. Be present and alive to this moment. See the beauty that is here; see the good that is already in your life.

Why would you want to set aside time to learn to meditate? So you become awareness itself – and in doing so, totally, fully, completely alive. It's worth it.

The True You, Beyond the Mind

Shifting your attention is the essence of being present and meditating. It is re-training your attention away from the thoughts of your mind. By doing that it breaks down the habit of unconsciously getting lost in, and believing, them. It is strengthening your "choice muscle." Being present gives you the ability to be aware and "detach" from thought; it allows you to pay attention to what you wish to pay attention to, it gives you freedom.

Being indifferent to your mind's objections, doubts, concerns, distractions and just being present with innocence, means you leave behind any sense of "what should be" and enter into that direct experience of what is – here is the experience of complete acceptance and focus and ease and contentment and peace and everything else that comes with giving up all the drama of the mind.

Furthermore, the more you tune into now, the more that quiet, restful, relaxed sense of awareness or presence (or whatever word you might use) will grow.

You're becoming familiar with the contents of your mind, but most importantly you're becoming more familiar with your own presence, your own state of being that is beyond any thought or feeling; the awareness that is the context to the content; the consciousness that is the core of you.

This natural state – that you were born into – is difficult to describe in a book. How would you describe your own presence? The quiet space of being that you might recognise from time to time? The experience of your existence, your aliveness, that unspoken, un-thought sense of "I am" within you?

Words just don't do experience justice.

It is a little like trying to describe a colour or what some food tastes like to someone. The experience of anything is beyond any words for it; words are just pointers. And that is important – you can think about it and have an idea about it, or you can jump in and discover the experience of it.

How nice would it be if you could immerse yourself in this experience, be present and aware easily, ending suffering and being nothing but calm, fun, focused and free?

Exactly ... very nice indeed.

Making meditation and being present a priority by setting aside the time to practice and become familiar with it, is worth everything. It is the single greatest thing you could do to live 200% of life.

The Best Way To Meditate Simply and Effortlessly

What is the best meditation technique?

The simple answer is the one that you actually sit down and do every day.

There are a million different ways to meditate. Try some and find one you click with; make sure you keep it simple and straight-forward. Try eyes open and eyes closed too.

It's possible to learn something about meditation from apps, or "how to meditate" websites and books; they're a great place to start. But nothing surpasses personal teaching.

You did say peace and happiness of some variety is *the* most important thing for you?

If you're serious about peace and happiness, find a teacher – someone who walks their talk, who lives 200%, who is peaceful and alive. Don't settle for less.

A teacher or coach who knows what they speak of is the fast path in any sphere of life. Meditation is no different. Get guidance from these people. They know what they're doing.

A valid meditation technique is valuable as it will focus the mind for you, with very little effort.

Not all meditation techniques are created equal. They are like cars. Some are fast, fun and easy to drive; others aren't. The technique has to be simple. The truth is simple, if it's not simple, it's not the truth. It is worth looking around.

I unreservedly recommend that you learn the Bright Path Ishayas' Ascension meditation techniques.

These are the techniques that I personally practise (every single day since 2003) and love to teach – but I am honest in my wish that you find quality teachers and a quality technique. I can hand on heart vouch for the Bright Path Ishayas and their integrity. I would not personally be an Ishaya if it wasn't so. Find them and learn Ascension.

Ascension may well be the most simple, effortless yet powerful meditation technique in the universe. Since you can use it with your eyes open, you can learn to be clear, calm and content, fluid and free, all day long.

I had been meditating for a while, but when I learnt Ascension it was like I had been stumbling around in the dark and all of a sudden someone turned the lights on – it made that much difference.

If you want the real deal – absolute, unbroken peace and happiness for the rest of your life, no matter what circumstances you're experiencing – you'll need more than any book can give you. Find a teacher. In fact, find a Bright Path teacher.[9]

Whatever you choose to do, simply sit and be at the centre of everything, watching, noticing, observing, being aware, just for this moment.

A child can sit and watch. So can you. And so you will, especially with practise.

This moment is the only moment you can do anything. The past is gone; the future not yet here. Just be here, right in the middle of the moment.

There are no problems here. All is well. Enjoy.

Just Do It

> *"The affairs of the world will go on forever.*
> *Do not delay the practice of meditation."*

> - Milarepa, Tibetan yogi

I know what a great thing being aware of the presence of now and meditation is, when it's regularly done, every day. The only way you're going to know is by proving it to yourself.

If you are committed to finding time, you will find time.

When you regularly practise, the benefits will become self-evident to you,

---

[9] See www.thebrightpath.com

and hence your commitment will develop a momentum of its own. But you need to make a start, so you can get to that point.

The fact is, if you make meditation and being present a priority, you will find countless times in your day when you can do it. How much of your day do you devote, say, to flicking through Facebook or watching Netflix or reading any old book?

If happiness and peace is a priority to you, you'll want to make time. You're doing what's important to you instead of frittering time away on what's not important.

Practise. Your commitment to peace and happiness and to leaving suffering behind is reflected in what you regularly do. Practise is key. If it's important, do it every day.

I probably don't need to tell you how rare walking your talk is in this world. It's a rare thing, but it's the only thing that gives you the results you want.

Make your practise times an essential part of your "to do" list. Schedule them into your diary.

Commit to these times – don't let them be flexible on some kind of "if and when I find the time" basis but a definite appointment. This way living 200% and living what is truly important to you becomes a reality in the shortest amount of time possible.

Wouldn't that be a great way to live?

A small amount of commitment and you'll have it.

Getting an Oasis of Calm and Clarity

When I first started the Bright Path Ishayas' Ascension, I was busy. As an outdoor instructor, my days were full on and always different, changing moment to moment. But since peace was a priority to me, and I was seeing definite results from this commitment, I increasingly made the most of moments I had to myself.

Maybe it was 10 minutes at lunch behind a tree, or when a group was late getting to me; whatever, whenever, I found the time to do it. It sometimes meant a sacrifice in that I didn't hang out with the guys and socialise quite so much, but it was worthwhile.

Finding time meant I had little "oases" of calm and clarity, little points throughout the day of detachment and recharge.

It meant I had more energy and more fun. I felt I was a better guide and teacher. I didn't come home totally wrecked from a hard day. I could switch off when I came home rather than thinking well into the evening about what happened in the day.

It meant peace and clarity wasn't just for a few moments after my morning practice. I "tuned in" regularly, and a sense of good attitude and energy, presence and fun soon became the norm throughout my day.

For sure, I'd hit bumps or get frustrated with a group or a fellow instructor, but I had a way of managing that too. It just didn't matter as much as it did before I started consistently practising.

Regular practise, spread throughout your day brings so much, I can't tell you.

Calm and Clarity for You and Everyone Else

I remember chatting with a lady who wanted to stop being so stressed. She, like many mums, was exhausting herself, constantly running around, constantly putting herself under so much pressure, and all so she could fully give to her kids.

Within five minutes, however, she was telling me she *needed* to be stressed because it meant she cared about her children. Taking time for herself was non-existent because it was "selfish."

This is a very important point – meditation and being present, aware and ending stress is not selfish. It's crucial for everyone around you, actually.

This time is for you to reconnect, recharge, to get to know your true state of peace and clarity, to become the best version of you. You are going to see that all of your life makes more sense and is easier after even 10 minutes of eyes closed practice.

It is only from this place of calm and clarity and with a full battery that you can really and truly help others.

It's not selfish at all. It's the most giving thing you could do.

Giving time to yourself means that you can absolutely give from a place of fullness and energy. It's worth repeating: when you are at 100% everyone benefits. You become a nicer, calmer, more fun person to be around. When you're at half-charge, you're half-arsed; nobody wins. You can't give to your full abilities, resentment or guilt comes in, you get grumpy, you get exhausted and stressed.

It doesn't need to be this way. Take the time out to give to yourself so you can give to everyone else. They will thank you for it.

Creating a Benchmark of Peace

*"What we plant in the soil of contemplation,
we shall reap in the harvest of action."*

- Meister Eckhart, German theologian and mystic

To be clear – meditation needs to be *lived*. It makes a difference in your life when it's a foundation for action, as an enabler for you to live fully, to perform at your best.

Being present and aware with your eyes open, when you're active, is an essential practice in itself. Diving into the presence of now with your eyes open *and* closed means you're making a pivotal choice in making sure your peace and happiness is a lasting reality.

You see, when peace is a conscious priority like this it starts becoming obvious when you *aren't* clear, calm or content, when you start getting muddled, frantic and dissatisfied.

The regular practice of showing up to now – eyes open and closed – sets a benchmark of calm so it's easier to know when you're getting wound up and you need to back down.

Without this benchmark, stress just creeps up on you. Sometimes you're not aware of how uptight you're getting simply because most stress comes in bit by bit, a death by a thousand cuts.

You don't notice how loaded down you are until that final straw comes that breaks the back, and you actually do your lower back in (a common stress-based psycho-somatic injury) and/or you snap and yell at the person who (often) least deserves it.

If you are regular with your choice to return to being present and of stopping and meditating, you're constantly resetting back to calm and clarity. You are teaching your body and mind that this is the new normal, not anything else.

With this baseline of calm, you are more able to take action to stay there. You are more conscious of your physical wellbeing, your internal attitude and mood, your energy, everything.

It means during the day, your baseline becomes easier to return to. If you fly off the handle, you can let go and reset quickly. You fly off less, need to apologise less; you put your body under less stress-based strain. Everyone is happy.

The bottom line is the ability to act – to have clarity of choice – as opposed to reacting, habitually.

There is nothing better than the ability to consciously steer your life in the direction you wish it to go. There is no need to be captive to the ups and downs of life. You want to be captain of your own ship, and you can be; it simply requires a little practice.

Knowing When You're About To Go Too Far

When you do fly off the handle, when you snap, lose it, react, say things you regret … it hasn't just happened. It's been developing some momentum over time, you just haven't been aware of the build-up – until it's too late.

Here are five things – internal "early warning" signs – that watching out for will show you when you are NOT prioritising your peace and starting to lose it. Being aware of these signs means you can bring yourself back before you explode messily.

The Five Key Things To Watch for:

1. Levels of calm/stress/agitation

Monitor your levels of calm and stress throughout the day. Remember: calm and stress has little to do with WHAT you are doing (i.e, the situation you find yourself in) and everything to do with HOW you're doing it.

If you meditate in the morning you'll have a nice benchmark to work from for the day. A session in the afternoon means you can settle back down, and go from there. An evening meditation means you can fully switch off from the day, enjoy whatever you have planned, get a good night's sleep and start afresh the next morning.

2. Negative thinking/resistance

Notice your internal dialogue – if it's getting negative, it's an excellent sign you can make another choice. Maybe it's just walking away to take a break and get another perspective. Maybe it's not letting the voice win and doing what you need to do anyway. Whatever it is, being aware of that voice and how it affects your peace is super useful.

3. Being hasty

You can only do one thing at a time. Recognise when you're starting to race around, trying to do several things at once. Stop, slow down, take some time to breathe, come back down and get present. "Less haste, more speed" as my Nan used to say.

4. Past/future thinking

You need to learn from the past and plan for the future (or enjoy and dream). No problem.

Recognise though when you're way wrapped up in the past and future. An excellent sign is when you're thinking about something you have no control over, or starting to be dissatisfied or frustrated with your current situation, or staring out the window thinking about the weekend or your holidays.

Instead of getting involved in those thoughts, come back to the same place as your body and focus on what's right in front of you.

5. Not having fun anymore

When you're getting serious, stop and change your attitude. It's a great signal that you're thinking too much; that peace-wise things are going down the plughole.

Take a break, come up for air, get perspective. Nothing in life need be serious; and it's all so much easier when you aren't.

Sometimes asking yourself, regardless of the situation you find yourself in, "How can I enjoy this more?" will give you a better idea of what to do.

Let all the above be great signs that you've stopped prioritising your peace. The sooner you catch them, the sooner you can change your internal state. Making that choice simple and automatic all comes from practice.

What Do You Do When Life Gets Tough?

It's all well and good if I say there are no problems here, and maybe you can experience that right now, but what happens when you forget and get stuck in suffering? What do you do when stress or fear or whatever has you fully in its grip?

The crucial thing is: the more present you can be in your everyday life, the easier it's going to be when things get tough. You'll notice yourself losing your cool and be able to step back and gain some objectivity sooner and sooner.

Consider that it's like getting fit: it's only by doing the training that you're able to run a marathon without feeling beaten up and being out of action for days, even weeks, afterwards. It's also like putting aside savings in a bank: only because you've made the investment are you able to get through the tougher times. You have resilience because you've invested in it.

The more you prioritise your peace, the more you can see it slipping – the more you can tell when you aren't prioritising it. It becomes super obvious when you stray from it. It just gets easier and easier to return. It actually gets to a point where peace comes and gets you when you leave it. Which, needless to say, is pretty cool.

So, don't let up on your practice when the going is good.

It's such a common mistake. Don't assume you don't need your practice. You need that ability, that fitness to choose when life gets tough. Practise and get so familiar with inner stillness that you never leave it, even when the house is burning down around you.

Being calm and clear starts with a choice, now. If you're consistent with that choice, being consistently calm and clear comes quickly, easily and simply always, no matter what.

But if you *are* frazzled and feeling like you're going to snap? Three things:

1. Stop

Just stop what you're doing. Don't try and get through whatever you're doing and then get some perspective back. Put the brakes on, and take a moment. Take as many moments as you can get away with. You'll always have at least one moment if you make one.

Breathe as deep as you can. Really get present and out of your head. Notice your body, notice if the stress is creating a physical reaction within you. Bring your attention to it, don't be it – feel it. Notice the story around the stress but don't get wrapped up in it again.

The Bright Path Ishayas' Ascension Attitudes are particularly good in these times – when you give them 100% of your attention. Gently, but fully bring your attention away from the stress and to the techniques.

Talk to someone – maybe the one causing the stress; maybe someone else. Just chat it through and get them to help you back to peace and calm, to get perspective. You don't want advice so much on how to fix the problem, simply on how you can deal with it better – that is the most important thing, although if a solution comes from it? Wahey – bonus!

Get some space and perspective back and then head back into what you were doing. You'll be amazed how a few minutes or even just moments can make a world of difference.

2. Don't be afraid of emotion

The inner critic can judge you harshly for being emotional. But anger, for example, can tell you a lot about yourself, about what is important.

Don't assume being peaceful and happy means never getting excited or passionate.

The only problem with something like anger occurs when you don't say what you need to say *when* you need to say it. Then it builds and builds and really explodes.

This would happen to me all the time: I'd have something to say to someone, and I'd second guess it, thinking that I was wrong anyway, or that it didn't really matter, that I could just let it go.

Well, as I found on countless occasions, it did matter and I couldn't let it go.

I didn't say what I needed to say and it just ate me up on the inside for a long time after. I got so angry and frustrated at the other person, and at myself, and it would build way out of proportion to what had happened.

It's far simpler to say what is there, in the moment. Even, and especially, if you think your voice might shake when you say it. Then you know it's really important.

> *"You can never embarrass yourself by speaking vulnerably.*
> *It is the path of champions."*
>
> - Jeff Brown, self-help author

It'll take courage, but the pain of a possible hit to the pride in the short term (by perhaps being wrong or that whole, "What will people think of me?") is nothing compared to anger and regret eating you up on the inside.

When you feel strong words or emotions coming, be very aware and see what it's all about. Be as clear as possible with your communications; don't hold back what you need to say, and then ... let it go.

By letting it go I mean be alive to this moment; don't carry the past.

You need to let it go. You need to be okay with the person not changing, not getting it. The crucial thing is you said what you had to say.

If you don't speak and/or you hold on to being right, you're only hurting yourself. Trust me, I know this one from a lot of experience.

You're not going to master this straight away, but keep doing it and you will get better and better. It will be easier and easier to be honest and clear.

Don't shrink away from challenging situations; don't avoid doing what you need to do. They only become stressful because you would rather they weren't happening, and you try to put them off. Don't avoid – accept the challenge.

You're always going to discover more about yourself, and sometimes the tough times show you the most. The best attitude when you see one coming? Say to yourself: "Excellent! Bring it on!"

Go lightly with this, okay? Don't take it seriously now.

3. Don't judge yourself

When you've gone through a stressful situation, the most important thing is to let it go as soon as you can. The sooner, the better. Let go of all the mental reviewing of what just happened. Just don't even get started on that track.

Tough times mean you have to stay present; otherwise, the critic in your head is going to give you a good kicking. What happens is that we stumble through an argument, for example, and then we look back and replay the whole thing with what we "should" have done or said.

Hindsight is a valuable thing, but you did what you did and that is that.

If you need to apologise, you go and say sorry, but again, the most important thing is to let it go. It's done. Know that you did your best and give it another shot next time. You can't do anything about it now, so give yourself a break and start fresh.

There is no value in endless recycling the past – but that is what will happen unless you stay out of your mind and are super present, alive to this moment.

Don't be tempted to think about it; it really cannot help. There is no value in the rehash.

What Do You Do When Things Really Fall Apart?

"When you're going through hell, keep going."

- Winston Churchill, former British Prime Minister

When it's all falling down around your knees, what do you do?

The one thing you need to do when you have a shock in life – whether it's the end of a relationship, the death of a loved one, losing a job, whatever – is stay out of your head.

It's not going to be a helpful place to be in right now.

The emotional shock of the event is one thing, but the ongoing analysis, the dredging up the past, the fear and uncertainty for the future – all of that – can create a downward spiral of more and more unhappiness.

It might seem like you can work out why it happened by thinking and thinking about it, but you can't. Your mind is not your friend in these moments; there is no clarity there, so stay out of it. Keep coming back to the present moment.

Fully experience this moment in time. If you want, use your body to "sense" this moment. What smells are there? Sounds? Sensations? Go into the world around you. Be right where you are, right now. Breathe deep – notice the air coming in and out, in and out. If you have learnt the Bright Path Ishayas' Ascension techniques, use them. Bring all your attention here; see what unfolds now.

The present is your saviour. Now, everything is manageable. Now, it is just what is in front of you, just one step at a time.

Don't get into your head. Don't indulge in the past or future. Don't listen.

Obviously, alcohol and/or drugs are easily available distraction options but, if abused, will just add to your miseries.

Tap into quality friends, those who won't let you wallow; talk with them, a lot. Exercise, walk, meditate, sing, spend some time with small children, play an instrument, bake, garden, get out in nature. Matt Haig in his book on depression, *Reasons to Stay Alive*, talks about the importance of beauty, and it's the same with any unhappiness:

"Wherever you are, at any moment, try and find something beautiful.
A face, a line out of a poem, the clouds out of a window, some graffiti,
a wind farm. Beauty cleans the mind."

Whatever you choose, choose something; do anything but listen to the voices in your head.

There will be emotions. That is okay. Emotions can be there, no problem.

Accept them; just don't get lost in them. Re-read the chapter on acceptance. See the difference between noticing the experience of the emotion and getting into the mind's story about the emotion. It is always the story that hurts, that ends in chaos.

It's no different if the emotions are particularly intense. Accept them – embrace them even. Just don't try to resist them if they are there. Try not to add more emotion to the emotion; i.e, don't be anxious about the anxiety, depressed about the depression, angry about the anger.

The worst thing about emotion is the judgement that it shouldn't be there. Or the "Oh no, here it is again, will I ever be free of it!?" kind of thoughts. Don't put yourself under any pressure. Let the emotion "float" – don't try and do anything about it. Don't resist.

Again, don't engage in any story. Just be very present. All stories will have a past and/or future element to them, and it is the story about the emotion that is the kicker, not the pure experience of the emotion itself.

So, accept: witness the emotion as it is in this exact moment. You can have an unspoken attitude of "What is this all about?" and just be with it.

Don't push it away; don't get lost in it. Simply see what is there to experience. In acceptance and awareness it will come and it will go much more simply.

Especially if there is guilt or regret combined in there it may take a little courage to be with the emotion, experientially. Nonetheless, come face to face with it and see it for what it is. When you do that, you will see that you don't need to hide from it or resist it, that you can be with it and it doesn't end in chaos. It's the resistance that creates the problem. It always does.

The emotion will go. It will change. Everything does.

Don't give yourself a timetable. The emotion, the situation – it's not going to last forever, but you aren't in control of when. Stay out of the "I should" thoughts, as in "I should be feeling better now …" Take the pressure off and just allow change to come through in its own good time.

As the adage rightly says, "This too shall pass." You will come through; you will be alright.

The Wisdom of Difficult Moments

"Difficulty shows what men are. Therefore when a difficulty falls upon you, remember that God, like a trainer of wrestlers, has matched you with a rough young man. Why? So that you may become an Olympic conqueror; but it is not accomplished without sweat."

- Epictetus, Greek philosopher

All you can do is take one step at a time. The only thing you know for real is what is happening right in front of you. Everything else is a guess.

That is the beauty and the wisdom that can be found in these times – you only have this moment. Make the most of it.

You get to see what a nightmare your head can be. It's a blessing, actually. Your mind has always been this way, mercurial, your best friend and then your worst enemy, and now your mind has an excuse to really spin out.

Sometimes miserable times in our lives can be the impetus so we learn to never go back down there again. If there is a lesson in any of this for you, let it be that. Let it be about learning to be more free.

You are finding a way of staying independent of your thoughts, to be the master of your mind and your reactions. You are finding your way to being so internally stable that no event can rock your peace; you are finding your way to living life continuously in this moment.

So practise now, even if the going is good, so you can style through the tough times.

You will come to a place where life makes sense. Where everything is easy, and fun, and fluid. And your mind just doesn't have the same grip over you anymore. Where pain still may happen, but you are completely free from suffering.

This place is true. It's the only true thing in the whole world.

CHAPTER FIFTEEN

Choice 7: To Be Bold
(when you want to blend in)

"I've never seen any life transformation that didn't begin with the person in question finally getting tired of their own bullshit."

- Elizabeth Gilbert, author of *Eat Pray Love*

The Courage To See Clearly

We are great story tellers – the whole human race revolves around stories. From collective myths about origins and destiny, good and evil, and the "natural" order of things to your personal stories about yourself and your life and why you can and you can't – stories structure our lives in subtle yet powerful ways.

Breaking out of the limiting patterns and beliefs your culture, upbringing and past has provided for you takes courage. At some point you may come to realise what you took for granted as "truth" or as "natural" isn't anything of the sort – it is simply an agreed way of living and seeing the world that you soaked up from an early age.

When everyone else *seems* to be blending in and ticking along quite nicely, and it *seems* you're the only one questioning, the only one who wants to take a road less travelled, it takes courage to stand out and go your way.

But what else are you going to do?

Squash that inner knowing and conform to what you think you should be and do? That's been done by many before, for sure. Does it lead to a satisfying life? Not at all.

When you venture forth on your own path, one thing you will come to realise is that it never was "the Man" keeping you in your place.

The biggest source of limitation in life by far lies much closer than that – it always was, always will be, between your own ears. Because of your mind's ability to shape and filter *everything*, it has the ability to stop you from doing *anything*.

Being brave enough to poke your stories and test them for lasting truth is one of the most liberating things you can do. Taking stock is necessary if you want to live 200% of life.

"Am I truly living the life I want to live?"

"What am I not doing that I long to do?"

*"Do I **really** want to do this, or is it just an idle 'it would be nice' fantasy? Or is it something I think I **should** do?"*

"Is what I'm saying and doing actually in alignment?"

"What limiting thoughts, beliefs, or stories do I hold to be true that mean I'm living a life less than?"

When I shone a light on the stories I was telling myself about my life, I realised so much of it was indeed utter bullshit: fluff and excuses. Unconsciously maintained, it ensured there were large parts of my existence which I could safely hide away from, where I could delay, compromise and blame someone else, where I was taking zero responsibility.

It takes a lot of courage and humility to examine your dearly held beliefs and stories. In many ways you've believed them to be True. Yet when this "truth" is seen as it is – just an idea, a story, a belief you have held to be true – you can step beyond it into a much wider, deeper, richer experience of yourself and your life.

You free yourself up to align with what is really True – and how wonderful is that?

True Heroism

Looking within and learning to fully and freely exercise your choice in life is the most rewarding journey that any human being could ever embark on. The rewards for turning away from stress and limitation are instantaneous, and they allow you to see yourself and the result of your choices with even greater clarity.

Awareness is a gift. Your limiting stories and patterns of living become more and more obvious. This is an excellent thing.

I do get that this may not be a *comfortable* thing.

Buddha once said that the most heroic thing that anyone could ever do was face themselves:

"It is better to conquer yourself than to win a thousand battles. Then the victory is yours. It cannot be taken from you, not by angels or by demons, heaven or hell."

When you look at yourself honestly, go easy. Be clear and direct but don't judge yourself harshly if you feel you have failed in some way. What is judgement but the very thing that you are leaving?

At some stage you will become aware of poor choices. Wonderful. You did the best you could, at the time. Now you're in a different position. You now see clearer and know better, so you will do better.

Keep walking towards what you want. Keep moving; keep making the choices that bring real fulfilment and contentment – not just for some future moment, but now.

Never look back in regret. If anything, regret is an excellent sign of clarity, that you have moved on and up. If you weren't a better person already, you wouldn't feel regret – you see? You did your best, now you know more. Drop the regret, keep walking forward, keep improving.

Your dream, your vision for your life can be true. It can be true! So many people have this dream. So few are willing to make sure they experience it.

I've got it good in that I'm surrounded by people who remind me of my dream for my life every time I see them. Their aliveness, their gratitude, their humility, their presence reminds, motivates and inspires me, constantly.

You may live with people like this or you may not, but you can be surrounded by them if you seek them out – for example, the internet has made the world a smaller place – but I bet they are closer than that. All it requires is for you to reach out and ask for help.

Reaching out and getting what you need is so simple, but how often do you?

Do it. Do whatever it takes to keep every moment filled with your dream. Do whatever it takes to stay inspired.

Be your own hero.

Passion and Purpose – What Aren't You Doing?

> *"I don't believe people are looking for the meaning of life as much as they are looking for the experience of being alive."*
>
> - Joseph Campbell, author of *The Hero's Journey*

What exactly is your dream? Your vision for your life? Have you ever wondered what your purpose is? For what reason you are on this planet?

I think many people spend their whole lives looking for their purpose. They want to find out why they are here. They want to wake up in the morning with a sense of reason, of being a part of something, of contributing to something, of knowing that they are of use.

The answer to your life's purpose lies in the question:

> *What makes you come alive? What is it that you love to do?*

The things that make you come alive are the very things that shape your purpose. Get clear on your passions and your gifts, and you'll find your purpose.

For you see, passion is like a GPS located in your heart; it gives rise to direction. Author Joseph Campbell once said:

"Follow your bliss. If you do follow your bliss, you put yourself on a kind of track that has been there all the while waiting for you, and the life you ought to be living is the one you are living."

Passion serves to show you what you should do most of in life. Where your interest is, your purpose lies.

The Boldness It Takes To Be Truly Alive

"To invent your own life's meaning is not easy, but it's still allowed, and I think you'll be happier for the trouble."

- Bill Watterson, *Calvin and Hobbes* cartoonist

It's one of toughest things too – it takes a certain boldness to actually start living your passion and purpose.

You actually already know what your passion is, you do; the hardest thing is that you feel you should be doing something else. It's that old chestnut of "who I am is not good enough" – what you want to do, you shouldn't.

Most people are waiting for some kind of permission to do the things that bring them the greatest joy. You know what you love to do. Are you waiting for the acknowledgement that you are *allowed* to do it, that it's *okay* to do it?

If so, here it is:

You are officially allowed to do whatever it is that makes your heart sing. God definitely wants you to; that's why she gave you a heart in the first place.

Chances are you don't think that what you love to do is enough, as in "useful" enough. You think it's too simple, not important or grand enough to make a difference. Or you want to do it more, but you doubt your abilities, or you doubt you can make a living doing it, or whatever.

Whether you are any good at it or can make money from it is irrelevant. Find as much time as possible to do it.

Because – when you do what you love to do, what state do you enter?

Aware, absorbed, excited, peaceful, complete, content, joyful, satisfied ... Alive.

The fact is you need to do the things you love to do because they make your life worth living.

Even if it means doing a job that isn't so great but that pays well or is flexible and gives you the time to go and do what you love: do it.

Do it so you can do what you love more, simply for the reason that you love it and it makes you live well. In the doing you may just find that you make the world a better place.

"Don't ask yourself what the world needs – ask yourself what makes you come alive, and then go do it. Because what the world needs is people who have come alive."

- Harold Thurman, American civil rights leader and theologian

That experience of alive presence and stillness that comes when you're immersed in what you love will show you the real key to purpose.

All doubt about what you want to do is dissolved when you fully give yourself to it. When you're absorbed in your own presence and awareness, when you stop worrying and start being, there is no doubt.

That is your real purpose: to come alive to such a degree that doubt, worry, fear no longer exists.

Your aliveness speaks volumes, far more than words or noble deeds. It changes people; it wakes them up. They notice your alive presence and want to really live too.

Your purpose is to be alive, truly alive. Fill every moment of your life with aliveness.

Be bold, follow your passion, make a difference.

Passion Versus Obsession And Addiction

When you have an inner foundation in acceptance, appreciation, gratitude and presence and your passions are a cornerstone of your "outer" life, you find constant fullness, everywhere you turn.

You are so alive doing what you love, that you love the simple fact of being alive. Loving the simple fact of being alive means everything you do, you love. Your inner foundation is strong. Contentment is everywhere.

Yet this is such a rare skill. I see so many who don't have that but instead have it all back to front.

There is a vast difference between following your passions so you are more alive and grateful for all of your life, and *relying* on your passions to make you alive.

There are many – obviously I see it a lot in the outdoors community because I know it well, but in all aspects of life – whose reliance on some activity indicates serious addiction issues.

They are fully in, obsessed, living their passion as much as possible. But there is no balance. Their jobs and relationships suffer. There is no foundation. There is no contentment anywhere else. They are lost, chasing happiness and aliveness, but also meaning, as much as any drug addict.

Witness the extreme nature of some sports fans. The highs when their team wins. The despair when "we" lose. It's not a hobby or entertainment any more, it's life and death. It's the search for aliveness, connection, identity and meaning solely on the outside, which is always doomed to fail.

In a similar sense, athletes of every calibre often struggle when they retire. What they were doing gave them something they cannot replace easily, simply because they don't know where to look. Depression is a real issue for many.

I've been talking about sports here, but the same applies in any field or community – business, music, art, relationships, meditation, politics, diet, fitness, anything.

In the chase for aliveness you have forgotten – or didn't know to begin with – that:

It isn't the things of life that bring you happiness;
it is you who brings happiness to life.

Addiction only comes because you believe the completeness of experience – aliveness, absorption, the Zone, etc, – can only be found in the thing or activity you desire.

You have bought into the belief that what you want most of all from life only comes from what you love to do. When you do "x" that, and only that, will make you happy. You won't be happy any other time.

I know this because I headed down that track for some time.

I didn't think or talk about anything beyond kayaking and the next trip. I had an almost physical itch when I hadn't been in a boat for a few days. I could find no enjoyment in the slightest "off" day on the river. I started having the worst attitude towards myself when I wasn't performing well, even though I was doing the thing that I said I loved. It became so there was no middle ground, no balance, no simple joy.

It all got a little extreme before I realised I needed to give myself a reality check. I did not want to live that way.

It's ironic – in your search for absorption, you are the furthest away from it than you have ever been.

It is one thing to have a strong desire to do what you love, and it is essential to live your passions. But only so your passions mean that you love *all* of your life more.

Be aware that if there is any lack of contentment in daily life, it means the balance has tipped. The desire starts to become an addiction and a curse and not an addition to your life. In addiction, nothing else satisfies.

Being addicted only leads to resentment, to an indifference to everything else.

In addiction, you aren't present – you are constantly in the future, in the next thing. Even when you are doing the thing you love, it has to be more than the last time; it has to be better, bolder, bigger – otherwise there is disappointment, boredom, restlessness.

Whether you realise it or not, everything is affected by this addiction because everything is pushed aside. You aren't present to anything else: if you can only be happy pushing some kind of boundary, you will only be happy a small part of the time.

What you are looking for – satisfaction, immersion, absorption, completeness, meaning, whatever – does not come from the task or the situation; it always comes from your approach to the task or situation.

It's not what you do, it's how you do it.

You need to learn to be fully present, to disconnect your happiness from the task so you can fully enjoy every experience: even the downtime, the times where you aren't on the "job" or aren't fully firing at the peak of performance.

The fact is that each and every moment of your life can be alive, underlined by sweet absorption and completeness, regardless of what you are doing.

Letting go of what has been and what will be is the key.

Just now – be awake and present. Be right here where your body is. Notice. Be fully involved in now. This never goes anywhere. It needs nothing. It is satisfaction and aliveness itself; and it's always been here.

Balance your passion for more with the reality of being alive in this moment. Don't miss out on the goodness that is here by the anticipation of future goodness.

Remember innocence?

Learn to find satisfaction and fullness of experience in the simple things, then everything will be so much greater. Learn to live a life of 200%, and then everything you do will be alive and full and rich.

Returning to my passion of whitewater kayaking recently has shown me the gains of 200% very clearly. There's a fundamental difference between me back then, and me now.

Now I have the ability to choose for the fullness of each moment, there is a real wow "I'm Alive!" factor, even on the simplest of rivers. There is contentment and joy first; it isn't given by the river or doing "good."

I definitely love kayaking, it gives me so much, but I'm not lacking anything anymore. I don't need the kayak to give me anything. Back before learning to meditate and be totally present I absolutely was missing the crucial element to, well, life itself. Not any more, I'm happy to say.

Be Bolder Than Your Comfort Zone

"Take action. Every story you've ever connected with, every leader you've ever admired, every puny little thing that you've ever accomplished is the result of taking action. You have a choice. You can either be a passive victim of circumstance or you can be the active hero of your own life."

- Bradley Whitford, American actor and political activist

If you never did anything different, where would you be?

If you never took a step into the unknown, what experience would you have?

The same as always, the same as everyone else.

I understand that sometimes it's easier to tell yourself that you can't change or leave a situation. Sometimes it's easier to accept and take the path of least resistance, I know. But the only way for you to really live a life of 200% is to have the courage to make different choices.

Everything that you have done that was worth doing has required you to go beyond your comfort zone. Moving forward is rarely comfortable.

The mind hates progress for this reason. And it's why you can use that feeling as a gauge to indicate what is truly important to you.

As author Steven Pressfield explains in *The War of Art*, if the idea of doing something makes you nervous, brings up doubt about whether you are up to the task, or makes you think, "I wonder what other people will think of me?", then that is an excellent indicator of importance.

Follow that idea; do that thing.

If something doesn't require you to overcome at least some internal resistance to get it, it probably has little value to you. The more resistance, the more value it has to you. As Steven Pressfield points out: "The opposite of love is not hate but indifference." He continues:

> *"Are you paralyzed with fear? That's a good sign. Fear is good.*
> *Like self-doubt, fear is an indicator. Fear tells us what we have to do.*
> *Remember one rule of thumb: the more scared we are of a work or*
> *calling, the more sure we can be that we have to do it."*

I don't think you will ever get to a place where courage isn't required. You just get better at dealing with it. You get better at ignoring the voice that says "I can't," the even more subtle "I'm not ready yet," and of course the "It might all go wrong and then what?"

Being bolder just seems to be a skill that, if you want more, you just have to practise. It starts with awareness of where your mind sets a boundary or a limitation and then setting your focus beyond these complaints.

What do you want to do? Expect resistance and jump anyway.

The first step before flying is to leap.

> *"Whenever there is fear, never try to escape from it. In fact take hints*
> *from fear. Those are the directions in which you need to travel.*
> *Fear is simply a challenge. It calls you: 'Come!'"*

> - Osho, spiritual teacher [10]

---

[10] A 2018 documentary stirred up controversy about Osho and his ashram. Nonetheless, his words have always rung true to me.

Risking Failure

Failure. When you lose. When you quit, ashamed, with your dreams in tatters, and all because you weren't good enough.

Yuck. Even just writing that sentence was a bit nasty.

And the consequences of failure – how the mind tends to focus on what could go wrong!

How you will be poor and penniless in the streets, how you will die alone, how you're actually going crazy and *will* end up in the mental hospital – all of these mad yet tempting future scenarios – can be a real source of fear and inaction: when you believe it, when you give it juice and it gets bigger, more real.

Fear of failure is one of the reasons people don't reach their goals and live their purpose.

It's everything we've talked about in this book: all the reasons why you may have great ideas and dreams but never get around to doing anything – the comfort zone, the self-doubt, the fear of what will go wrong.

But fear is what your mind will give you.

Your mind will tell you: "Don't risk failing, then your dreams can never be ruined. Don't risk anything, keep a hold of what you've got."

Playing safe and comfortable seems like a good idea, to your mind – but it never is. If you never risk, your dreams stay that way. You get to the end of your life having never made your ideas a reality; they stay as fluffy clouds in your head. You never live your purpose, you never truly live at all.

Risk is necessary. But with risk, I'm not talking about being irresponsible, I'm not talking high-risk gambling with finances or life and limb. I'm talking about not being afraid of fear, of testing your comfort zone. What you will see, however, is the more you test your comfort zone, the more you will come to re-define what your mind suggests is irresponsible.

Understand that the scale of that risk is completely up to you – don't let anyone pressure you.

One of the proudest moments of my life (in hindsight) was walking away from a bungy jump.

I was terrified but really wanted to do it. They strapped me in, did the count down, and ... I didn't jump. The operators counted again, again I hesitated. They mocked me, told me to "strap it on." Needless to say, that wasn't the right approach.

I was ashamed as I walked away, the jump untaken, but later I was proud of myself.

Jumping off any height is a huge deal for me, and I wanted the experience to be something (for want of a better word) "beautiful." The conditions weren't right, and so, despite the pressure, walking away was the only option.

Risk – and fear – is an extremely personal thing.

Becoming more aware of your fears, your resistances, your limitations, and choosing to do something even slightly different in *any* sphere of life, *is* a bold and beautiful thing. Truly.

Setting aside the fears of my mind and focusing on what needs to be done to get down a hard rapid in my kayak is a beautiful thing (to me), but so was over-coming my fears about commitment and fully committing to my now wife. That took a serious leap, just as running rapids does.

Being a father involves risk as well: "What if we're doing it wrong?" There's so much conflicting advice and personal experience out there about everything, not to mention your own intuition – you just have to choose a path that seems right to you. You just have to leap.

No matter what part of your life you meet fear in, no matter what your perception is of the scale of your steps forward, give yourself a pat on the back for facing it. Well done for accepting the true invitation of fear and risking being curious about what is on the other side. It's not easy, I know, but it is rewarding.

So – take encouragement and inspiration from others, but not pressure. You may never throw yourself off a bridge with an elastic band attached, and you don't have to if you don't want to. Now I've realised all I have about risk, I probably will never try bungy jumping again. I don't need to.

The Courage To Make Mistakes

"The price of inaction is far greater than the cost of making a mistake."

- Meister Eckhart, German mystic

Going beyond your fear of failure means you *have* to risk making mistakes. To do *anything* you have to risk making mistakes.

The fact is, the only way you learn, the only way you get better, the only way you can master anything is by trying and practising things that you are not good at currently. In this, you *will* make mistakes. Without mistakes you cannot learn anything.

Some years ago, I read an interview with a pro-snowboarder. She said: "If you're not falling, you're not trying. If you're not trying, you will never improve." From then on falling on my arse was seen in a totally different light, and not as further proof that I was useless and might as well quit.

This doesn't just apply to sport but also to any and every sphere of human endeavour: in business, art, relationships, parenting, dieting, quitting addictions, being more courageous, being a better human.

Mistakes are a part of getting better. Don't be afraid of them.

Now, having said that – if you find yourself making the same mistakes over and over again, there's something crucial that you're missing. You need to look at that or, even better, get someone's help. An outside view, impartial to your stories, is incredibly valuable.

But mistakes can be uncomfortable, can't they? Very uncomfortable, sometimes. Getting someone to help you with mistakes? Extremely uncomfortable. No wonder so many are content to stay safe and comfortable, and yet never improve.

If you have the right attitude you will embrace mistakes, you might even get *excited* about them.[11]

---

[11] Bizarre, I know – but true!

You see – a mistake is simply where the light of awareness shows you the cockroaches in the room: if you look, it shows you the limiting beliefs, habits, judgements, patterns at play.

Cockroaches don't like the light, they run and hide from it. With mistakes, shame and self-violence can come in which means you don't investigate further. You don't get to the cause, you just focus on what went wrong, and how stupid you are, again. You don't learn from your mistakes. You either keep doing the same thing, or clam up, and never risk making a mistake again.

I remember once beating myself up for some perceived sin. After a while I managed to open up and talk to a Bright Path Ishaya friend and colleague whose opinion I respected very much.

He showed me that when you make a mistake you can choose to get excited – or at the very least curious: "I *see* you!" "I see you!" means you can now do something about what was previously invisible. "I see you!" means in the inner game you have the upper hand against your opponent, those cockroaches. "I see you!" means you now have choice.

How To Re-Define Failure

Mistakes and failing are a *necessary* part of mastery.

If that is the case, and indeed it is, is there really any such thing as a "mistake"?

I know all the things that I have done that I was ashamed of have shown me, in stark light, something valuable. Instead of hiding away, it's been essential to get back on the horse and try again.

With the right attitude – of acceptance, of the silver lining, of awareness – mistakes aren't backward steps. They are springboards, and they can help you take giant leaps forward.

You will have to be supremely present and humble, but all of the choices in this book involve humility and a sense of humour, don't they?

Now, you've made a mistake ... something has turned out "wrong" and you can't shake it from your mind – it's putting the boot in over it. You may be trying to embrace your mistake, "I see you!" ... but around and around it cycles in your head.

The more you practise meditation and being present, the more you will be able to see the silver lining, let it go, and start fresh. It really is a boon in every way to end regret and guilt and self-violence.[12]

However, if this is impossible to you right now, talk to someone you trust. No one around? Don't want to talk?

Paul Mort, the life and business coach, uses a very useful tool to help be present and get some distance, end the despair of "messing up," and see the silver lining.

Sit and simply write down everything that happened, as objectively as possible. Be as present as possible, don't get into a story or the emotion about it. Get it all down on paper.

Once all the facts are down, draw a line under them. This is the story, it is the past, it is what has happened. It's time to move on.

Now detail what you might do differently next time you are in the same situation or embark on a similar project, or whatever it is.

---

[12] How's your practice going?

Be present, ignore any attempts of your mind to drift back into the past, and ask yourself: what have you learnt? Is there anything you can do now? What will you do next time? How will you make sure you do that?

Detail away, but when you're done, you're done. It won't take long. When you have the half-step back and are present, it'll be there pretty quick.

Then? Let it all go. Be here now, in this moment. Give yourself permission to be free to enjoy this moment and what is in front of you to the fullest.

It's a very handy tool as it helps you change the focus on what is wrong, from a past moment – and all the emotional and mental churning that goes with it – and shifts your focus to the lesson, to what you can do from now on.

It gives you distance from self-violence and it gives you a new, fresh future. It gives you optimism not despair.

Most importantly, it's not even really about the learning. It allows you to be present again – and that is the most important thing when you're going over any mistake or failure.

When you're aware, it doesn't take a lot of processing to learn from your mistakes; it downloads pretty quick, quicker than thought, way quicker than you realise. You know it, you recognise it, you're already "absorbing" it – learning done.

Going with your mind and thinking about it over and over again, trying to squeeze a lesson from it, trying to work out why you messed up again, really means fear has won, in a subtle way. It is fear's way of making sure you stay in a state of inaction.

It means you don't trust yourself or your ability to learn without too much input from your busy, fearful, doubting, regretful mind telling you:

"If you've done it once, you'll do it again" – you're already far into the future. It's a way of subtly punishing yourself for failing too.

And it means you've momentarily forgotten to prioritise your peace and contentment, no matter the circumstances you find yourself in. When you realise what you're doing? Jump back on the horse of presence.

There Is No Failure

The fact is if you have the courage to welcome mistakes, your approach to the whole of life changes.

It stops you being a victim, where mistakes are somehow life punishing you, evidence that you're "wrong again." Instead they become a valuable guide.

When you embrace mistakes, Life, the Universe, the Supreme Being, whoever or whatever it is that guides all of us and has our highest interests at heart – gets excited. When you finally take full responsibility for even your mistakes, when you really start *playing*, the Universe can show you all manner of cockroaches, all manner of limitations:

"Hey, see here, you can love more here. You can be more accepting here. You can be more present here. You can be more honest here. You can have more courage here ..."

Now life can give you exactly what you need. It can show you exactly what you need to see. And all you have to do is show up and be present and curious to it. Isn't that wonderful? You are not being punished, you are being *taken care of*. This is happening *for* you.

Your whole path to mastery and freedom is laid out, and you just take one step at a time. How reassuring – *if* you have the courage to embrace it.

In this, how can there be any such thing as "failure"?

Perhaps failure is best described as quitting because you are afraid of trying? To paraphrase the fitness coach and philosopher Pat Flynn again, the only failure in life is not trying; it is inaction.

The True Reason Behind a Fear of Failure

I've mentioned this previously, but it's worth repeating.

Being afraid of trying, being afraid of failure is so common. It's a big thing. One cause for a fear of failure is not appearing as good as you think you are, to yourself.

However, the biggest source of fear actually comes from what other people will think of you. Our mammalian brain's concern with social connection, of pecking order, is a huge inhibitor – if you let it be.

It's not so much fear of failure that puts the brakes on things, but fear of failing *in front of others*. You can pretty much fail all you like when there's no one around; put yourself on public display and it becomes a very different game.

A fear of failing in front of others stops you doing so much, simply because by doing anything you are putting your head above the parapet. There is no protection there, you can be seen from a million miles away – and you might be judged, you might get laughed at, you might be thought an idiot, you might make a huge mistake.

As I put the finishing touches on this book, I realise very soon people I respect will actually read it. I stand by every word, and yet I'm about to go public. Even though I know this fear well, clicking "send" to the publisher still takes a little something extra.

To do what you need to do and say what you need to say can be very uncomfortable, especially in the beginning; but this lack of comfort is so very necessary to come to terms with.

If you don't come to terms with this fear and the preference to stay comfortable, you simply won't do the things you say you want to do. You'll never get your questions answered or get your doubts allayed. You won't say the things you want and need to say. You won't live the life you want.

What if you never truly live your purpose or your passions or be yourself – all because you have a mistaken idea that something about you is wrong?

> *"All you have to do is follow through. Never give an inch to fear.*
> *Focus on what is real – never doubt, never turn from the One.*
> *Then, when you master that, life is simple."*
>
> - Maharishi Sadashiva Isham, Ishaya teacher

The Courage To Be Authentic

> *"If you want to improve, be content to be thought foolish and stupid."*
>
> - Epictetus, Greek philosopher

You're wrong, mistaken, backward?

That's not true, *at all*. Yet almost everyone has a fundamental belief: "I am doing it wrong. I *am* wrong."

They believe that everyone else is doing it right, everyone else knows what to do, and they are the only ones who are struggling and getting it wrong. So they follow the crowd.

It's because of this belief that many of us take care not to put a foot out of line, not to ask too many questions, not to stand out, or be honest and become a target – because if people see us they might see how wrong we are.

So instead we present an image, a pretence. We try to blend in, to be all things to all people. We think they're right and we're wrong. If there's a problem, it's our fault.

It takes awareness and courage to step outside these limiting patterns.

Yet what else are you going to do?

It takes so much energy to be someone else, to hide. Incredible peace and fulfilment comes from stepping beyond "What if I make a mistake?" and "What will other people think?"

It's also very inspiring to others. People notice and love it. They may not consciously recognise it, but on some level they do: "Here is someone who is real, someone who is comfortable and complete in themselves. Needing no approval, with nothing to hide, nothing to prove – and I want that for my life too."

So, do yourself, and everyone else, a favour. Have the courage to be real and authentic. When your heart starts hammering, do it, or say it. Needing courage can be an excellent GPS for living 200%, regret-free.

Choose To Have the Courage To Do Different Things ... or To Do the Same Things Differently

I'm all for having the courage to do different things. It's an important part of life, one that you'll get better at the more you do it. Note, however, that there are two aspects to making different choices. It's a crucial point because everyone focuses on the new and the different, everyone focuses on changing the outside world.

Everyone wants to pack it all in, run off to a tropical island, burn their phones. Everyone is good at pointing the finger and saying, "Well, I need to do something, something isn't working, so I'll change that, that and this; and while I'm at it, I'll ditch him and her ...", you know?

It's a whole new world to simply adjust your internal choices: to do the same things but from a different point of view.

Instead of ditching your phone, perhaps you could learn to use it and not let it use you? Instead of quitting a job you dislike, perhaps you could learn to adjust what you focus on? Instead of moving to a tropical island where you hope there's no stress, you could adjust the way you deal with stress now? Instead of splitting up with your partner perhaps you could change what you bring to the relationship?

Because if you don't have the courage to change your fundamental attitude and internal choices then it doesn't matter what different things you do: where you live, your partner, your job, whether you have a smart phone or not.

None of this matters because you will recreate the same problems, every time, simply because no matter where you go and what you do, you take your head with you – and your head is the source of all of your problems.

*"You are the only problem you will ever have
and you are the only solution."*

- Bob Proctor, self-help author and coach

Don't get confused with this.

Just because you *can* learn to deal with anything doesn't mean you *should*. If you want to make change, make change. But recognise if you don't change your internal choices you will recreate the same problems over and over again.

More often than not, a course correction in life starts with an internal change: doing the *same* things differently – with awareness and choice. That's where freedom lies, not so much in changing the outside world to suit you but changing your attitude first and foremost.

What Would You Do If You Knew You Couldn't Fail?

What would you do if you knew the future was going to turn out perfectly?

What if?

Keep the door of possibility wide open. Go beyond the voice that says you might fail, that something might go wrong, that you are not good enough.

The inner critic can only see limitation and problems; it cannot see potential and possibility. Infinity is far too much for the mind to grasp, and that is why it focuses on the small: on lack, what you don't have, and what might go wrong.

Believe in this and the world gets squashed and grey, and you along with it.

What if you flipped this lack thought? Do you ever focus on what might go right? That you are more than good enough?[13]

Why not?

Why not embrace an attitude of vision and of possibility? Instead of listening to the "You can't" or the "You won't," why not go with the "What if?" and the "How about?" ...?

Drop the limitations.

They are only imagined; they only have power because you believe them. Instead, focus on the possibility – the greatness of what could happen.

Assume an attitude that lights up your life, and in doing so lights up the lives of all those around you. Assume an attitude that everything will turn out just fine. Be grateful now that the future result is taken care of. Be supremely present in this knowing. How do you live now, knowing this?

Why wouldn't you? What have you got to lose? Wouldn't this one shift make your life amazing?

Attitude informs everything.

Possibility

There are those who live their lives as if nothing is possible, that nothing

---

[13] Hunt down English classical conductor Benjamin Zander and his talk *Work (how to give an A)* all about this. It's a great watch: www.youtube.com/watch?v=qTKEBygQico

much can change. Then there are those who believe that, even if in theory, anything is possible. What a difference it makes.

As the car manufacturer Henry Ford is often quoted:

"Whether you think you can or whether you think you can't, you're right."

Now a healthy cynicism is great. I'm not asking you to believe anything. But it is possible to be innocent, to be open, to believe that anything could be possible. It's not very scientific to refuse to be open to new or different things. You need to test them, to try them out, truly.

Ishaya teacher Maharishi Sadashiva Isham once said something very bold:

"Life is meant to be lived in eternal joy and infinite freedom and unconditional love and unbounded awareness. Any other life is utterly missing the point of being born a human."

He insisted that the birthright of every person is eternal peace, joy and bliss. That love is not an emotion, but your true nature. That not only is it possible to be completely free of suffering, but it is how you are supposed to live.

You can take two approaches to this:

That it's not possible, that he has lost touch with reality, or at least the common person's life, and his words are only for a select few.

Or, that seemingly amazing as his words are, everything he has said is indeed possible for anyone who puts their heart and mind to it.

Why not try and see? Would that not be better than stopping before you even start?

> *"Since death is inevitable, why not do as the sages say*
> *and see if what they say works?"*

> - Nisargadatta Maharaj, Indian spiritual teacher

I would so rather live with the door of possibility wide open. It's a very expansive way to live. It's so freeing to live from "What if?" It's so freeing to assume that there are no limitations other than those I impose on myself.

Choose to be open to anything at all happening, to hold nothing fixed, to hold no certainty except that magic is a possibility.

And that possibility *is* magic.

The Ultimate in Possibility

The biggest possibility for your life comes when you become aware of the nature of the most dominant yet subtlest story you have been telling yourself, the unconscious driver of all your limitation and drama – and one that has been reinforced by every single person you have ever met (because they believe it too):

You believe that you are broken.

You believe you are imperfect; that in some way, shape or form, there is something wrong with you. That you need to become in some way better, more complete before you are truly worthy.

You need to learn, gather more knowledge, discuss more – and then you can act, or truly be who you want to be.

You think you are climbing a mountain to a better state of being, to becoming a better person. A journey, a metamorphosis: progressing, schooling yourself, improving yourself.

That's what it feels like doesn't it? It feels like transformation happens because you climbed out of one state into a better, more advanced state.

Climbing a mountain is great when you're feeling great and all appears to be well. The trouble is it's horrible when it feels like hard going, when it doesn't appear to be going well. When you slip up, you feel like you fall back and lose that precious ground. Mistakes can seem almost life-threatening. No wonder we have trouble embracing them.

Sometimes the slippery mountain is so real it creates nothing less than an abject fear of falling into hell, and the desperate hope that one day you'll find heaven.

Sometimes you get so demoralised with the slipping, falling back into old habits you just give up:

"What's the point?!" you yell at the sky, and yourself.

"I'm never going to get there anyway!" as you throw away your intention, your goal, your vision for your life, for someday getting to the place you want to be and finally being the person you want to become.

I want you to consider something though.

The story you have been telling yourself is that you are lacking and need to get better. That fundamentally you are not good enough. To become worthy and "unbroken," the idea is you need to gain something and/or leave something behind.

It may appear like this, but in this "journey" it's very different.

The inner game is less about going somewhere and is actually more like what the Buddha said when he talked about walking a razor's edge. Ooh! Sounds dramatic doesn't it? But it's like a tightrope, a balancing act where, in order to get where you want, all you need do is just stay balanced.

To be more aware, more present, to transcend stress, negativity and limitation, to get to where you want, all you have to do is jump up onto now. You want to stop being mad or sad or bad? Just be aware now.

You fall off – of course you will fall off because like any skill you're not so good in the beginning; but what do you do? Just get back on. Be here, now.

You haven't lost anything. You haven't declined, this isn't a game of snakes and ladders – you just fell off. You just forgot. You fell asleep.

Now you're awake. Jump back on! Consistency you see. Get back on and do the things that you know you need to do – which in terms of transcending the limited part of you is simply stay alert to now and your presence within that.

Jump back on.

You'll stay there longer and longer and longer AND the things that make you fall off just get more and more obvious. You begin to master that fluid, simple, effortless focus of staying on until one day you find you're staying on much much more than you're falling off.

All because you made jumping back on more important than falling off. All because you got back up into that zone and ignored all those thoughts that said you've fallen back, you're useless, you might as well give up anyway.

What is even truer still, being free of stress, negativity, limitation and living calm, contentment and awareness is that it's not even a balancing act. It's more like you're soaking in it.

It's a hot bath. And the small you, the ego, your limited beliefs and patterns are like an ice cube. The things you don't know, the interferences that get in the way, they melt away just by immersing yourself in the presence of now.

When it comes to having a bath there is no right and wrong. There is just soaking in it. There are no mistakes, no failures – just reminders that you're out of the bath. It's through habit you jump out of the bath. In the beginning, a lot. *No deal!* You fell asleep. You just fell asleep.

Now you're awake, jump back in to the one place that really satisfies, and the one place stress, drama, negativity *can't* exist, and where everything you don't need melts away.

The more you jump back in? The more you realise just how pleasant this bath is. It never gets cold. It always has your favourite rubber ducky.

This bath is the one place where you are whole and complete. Not broken, *perfect*. It is where you are in the right place at the right time.

When you believe you are broken, that there *is* something wrong with you?

You've just hopped out of the bath. That's all. Come back in.

How "Not Broken" Changes the Outer Game

Mastering your limited beliefs, not waiting to be "better," being wide open to being ready and "good enough" right now ... it all means you have the inner foundation for improving at anything in the outer game.

Actually, soaking in the hot bath where there is nothing wrong with you also describes the best basis for learning and success in any field.

Dan John, the throwing and lifting coach (and religious studies academic), once said that success came from a three part process:

1. Show up (stop talking and start doing)

2. Don't quit

3. Ask questions

It's *just* like soaking in a bath. Get in, stay in, immerse yourself in the experience, support and community of those that have gone before you.

Since we believe we are broken however, we're not innocent. We're waiting – to become better, more worthy – and that creates fear and inaction, a lack of exploration.

You spend a lot of time talking about "wanting" to do it, you gather knowledge in preparation, but you never start. If you do make a start, procrastination is rife – you never show up consistently; you're afraid to stick your hand up and ask questions to get better.

You get despondent easily as – inevitably – something unexpected happens and you think you slide back down the mountain. Yet as Dan John explains, if he learnt one lesson in all his years of coaching, it is that:

"'The athlete quits the day before the great leap forward.'
Frustration, injuries, losing and failure are all opportunities to
learn more in sports ... and life ... It is what you do with failure
that makes you a champion."

You quit, right before the leap forward, to go look for something you're "good at," something you think you can do – which is code for "not fail at."

It's a wonder we learn anything from the level of a stressed, exhausted, busy head with its mind-wandering, resistance and blaming, doubt and confusion, anxiety and fear of failure, negativity and limitation, isn't it? And you can see the proof – notice how quickly young children master a host of different skills and abilities. Adults can rarely do that.

Being innocent and transcending the belief that "I am broken," combined with the commitment to just get back in the bath of experience, to give yourself time immersed in whatever thing you're learning, is an unstoppable force.

Okay? So don't wait. Stop talking and thinking about it, begin, and keep going. Jump back in.

Assume perfection and be whole – it changes everything.

Being Perfect Isn't Being Arrogant

"It takes courage to recognise that we are not victims to anything
outside of us. Recognising that we are perfect is one
of the bravest things we can do."

- Priya Ishaya

"Who am I to declare that I am perfect?"

It is a bold move, a bold move indeed, but has nothing to do with arrogance. It has nothing to do with evaluation, with progress, with being better.

Perfection isn't linear, it has nothing to do with learning or achieving goals, it has nothing to do with habits or the past or the future. It has nothing to do with anything your mind can conceive.

Perfection comes with the experience that there is nothing wrong with you. That yes, you will gather knowledge and wisdom, but that your fundamental nature is perfection itself – exactly as you are.

Witness a small baby. Is there any such thing as self-doubt or even self-confidence? It doesn't exist. There's no such thing. There's no inner struggle at all, and yet how much love, how much joy, how attracted are you to this little perfect being? What wouldn't you give to nurture, protect and guide them? They are so wonderful, so magnetic to us simply because they are so innocent and free.

My most memorable moments before learning to Ascend all involved this (all too temporary) absence of self-criticism, self-evaluation and self-management. Where I simply fell into a space – my true nature – of just being; a state of being that needed nothing, nothing at all.

So different from my other, mind-based existence of more or less constant striving and struggling.

Perhaps you know moments like these as well? Regardless, when you go beyond the mind's need to try and enhance, improve, secure and defend yourself, there you are – full and complete. Nothing needs to be done.

This is living a life of 200% – having the courage to let go of what the mind thinks it knows, what it fears, what it judges and believes. Giving up the struggle to become and secure, to edit and present an appropriate image, to manage and control; where you surrender to the innate goodness, the innate perfection that is within you, already.

In reading this book you may be seeking to become a better person. You've seen glimpses of being this person throughout your life, you want to make it permanent. Yet all you need to become this perfect person is to stop trying to be something you're not; rest in the presence that is already within you. You need do so very little but let go of the mind.

The Perfect Paradox

I get the paradox here, I do.

If you don't have a desire for self-improvement you won't do anything, you won't stay consistent and ever lose your chains and gain permanent peace. But if you don't let go of the mind's need to self-improve you won't find permanent peace, either.

American psychologist Carl Rogers once wrote,

> *"The curious paradox is that when I accept myself*
> *just as I am, then I can change."*

But you need do very little to change. You immerse yourself in the bath of now, and all of your limitations and habits dissolve, in the perfect time, giving you every experience and every lesson you need, as you need it.

Perfection is the unspoken experience when you stop climbing the mountain and just soak in the bath, in the presence of now, way beyond the limiting factor of your mind bringing self-doubt and lack into it.

You can only have that experience from within the bath, not from the outside. So jump in!

Soaking is the logical conclusion of all the choices so far: upward spiralling acceptance, appreciation, love, courage and full responsibility. You never stop choosing, but the choices we've outlined become your natural way of responding to life.

Having the experience of being in the one place where you need nothing, where nothing is wrong doesn't mean you don't do or say anything. It just means you do it with perfect authenticity. You do it without worrying about other people's expectations that you can't or shouldn't.

It takes extreme boldness to assume your perfection. When everyone else believes there is something wrong with them, when your mind believes there is something wrong with you, it is the opposite of blending in.

It isn't arrogance, it's just giving up that one belief that there is something wrong with you. It's the end of the ego – it only has a toe-hold when you don't love and accept yourself fully, exactly as you are right now.

It's giving up judgement of yourself. It's giving up the story that you are a victim to anything in life. It's giving up the past, giving up the hurts, giving up everything in exchange for resting fully in this present moment in time.

It isn't that you can't learn anything, that you won't evolve: it's that right now, immersed in your presence, there is nothing wrong. All is well; everything is perfect.

All is well, all is on track because there is no track, you are in the perfect place at the perfect time because now is life itself:

> *"Once you realize that the road is the goal and that you are always on the road, not to reach a goal, but to enjoy its beauty and its wisdom, life ceases to be a task and becomes natural and simple, in itself an ecstasy."*
> - Nisargadatta Maharaj, spiritual teacher

From that foundation all of life gets easier. You spend so much less energy trying to live up to your expectations of how you should be. Instead, you are. You know what is right for you and when. There is an incredible realisation of how your mind shapes everything you believe to be real – even who you think you are. The choice to get out of your thoughts and experience reality directly is obvious, clear, simple.

So, consider that a possibility – for it is the ultimate in possibilities – that you live life so immersed in the now bath, so beyond ideas of self-doubt, right and wrong, and the belief that "One day I'll be worthy," that perfection is realised.

Chances are you'll be so content you won't even realise it.

Stop Waiting

The beauty, the simplicity, the Truth is that you are already what you seek. Right here, right now. You *are* it.

Stop waiting.

It'll take courage. It will. I don't care how brave you think you are, this is the real test.

One of the most courageous things you can do is live like there is nothing wrong with you, that you are not broken, that you are more than enough.

Stop waiting. This is it. Stop postponing, stop waiting for a better future moment, stop waiting for a better future you.

Life is not a practice of becoming – even though you become.

Life is a practice of no-holds barred *living*, because there is no time like the present, because there is no better version of you coming in some better future moment.

This is it. Here You are. Grip the bull by the horns and dance, by the light of the moon if you like poetry, but dance now.

Don't sit on the sidelines, *waiting* ...

CHAPTER SIXTEEN

Choice 8: To Be Zero
(when everyone is telling you to be someone)

"When you make yourself into zero,
your power becomes invincible."

- Mahatma Gandhi, Indian political and spiritual leader

Make Yourself Zero

Often when people come to me to learn the Bright Path Ishayas' Ascension, they ask about what they are going to get. I usually say nice things like less stress and struggle, better sleep, more peace, rest, energy, focus, purpose.

But if they're really interested in where the road goes, I would tell them they get nothing. In fact, they lose many things.

When you dive into a true teaching you lose your positions, your judgements, your need to be secure, to control and to be right. You lose all your "shoulds." You lose all idea of what you think you are. Critically you lose the grip your mind has on you. It's the loss of these things that brings peace and potential, not the gaining of anything.

The German mystic Meister Eckhart put it perfectly:

*"God is not found in the soul by adding anything,
but by a process of subtraction."*

The undoing of all internal limitation reveals your true beauty and power beneath – the essence of who you already are, who you've always been but have been second guessing, trying and controlling to be someone you think you should be instead.

It's an interesting paradox – the whole world seems to be telling you to be someone, and yet your greatest peace and your greatest potential comes from reducing yourself to Zero, to nothing.

When you do that, a higher power, the big Self – whatever you want to call it; a much more wise, much more funny, much more compassionate force than your small self could ever try to be – can flow through you unimpeded, complete, without edit.

This is how you have the greatest impact on the world; not by being someone, but by being no one, by getting out of Your way:

*"The Universe is saying, 'allow me to flow through you unrestricted,
and you will see the greatest magic you have ever seen.'"*

- Klaus Joehle, author

Stop the Search, Quit the Fight

You probably already have had glimpses of these moments. It's not like it takes any amount of time. It certainly doesn't take any effort. Everything you need to live like this is already within you.

Like the clouds clearing, you've had the experience of pre-formed, pre-existing perfection: "Ahh ..." you say, "*This* is how life is meant to be lived"
...

This is it – this is the thing, the feeling, the experience, the unity, the perfect moment that everyone is searching for.

It's why you do what you love to do, it's why you love that feeling of doing something "well."

"Doing it well" is a tricky thing to put into words, but you know when it happens: Olympic champion or local athlete; principal dancer or weekend night-clubber; concert pianist or bedroom guitarist; master artist or hobby painter; everyone knows the internal "atmosphere" or sense of being in a state of Flow, in the Zone, in the now bath.

Anxieties are non-existent. There is no distraction or concern, only maximum presence, flowing performance. It is simple, totally fresh yet so clear, so obvious, so "known"; it is effortless, focused and supremely enjoyable. Here lies the source of all success and joy.

This internal experience is what brings us back for more, more than any other reward. Lives are changed by it. Flow can be intense, like a spiritual experience; and both come from the same source. A monk's dedication to the Supreme Being and a surfer's search for the perfect wave are only separated by context. Flow is the essence of humanity. It's how we were meant to live all the time.

It's why we work so hard, it's why we fight so hard too – why we control and strain and scramble for power or money or a soul mate or a gold medal or adventure or take drugs ... to experience the thing that, ironically, we already are.

It's the universal search of humanity and in our attempt to become better at it, we lose it.

We look everywhere, except within. Even those who look within don't look with innocence. They look with eyes of "I should" and "I need to become" – with predetermined ideas of what is right and what is wrong about themselves – and it's the greatest trap.

> *"All spiritual teachings are only meant to make us retrace our steps to our Original Source. We need not acquire anything new, only give up false ideas and useless accretions. Instead of doing this, we try to grasp something strange and mysterious because we believe happiness lies elsewhere. This is the mistake."*
>
> - Sri Ramana Maharishi, Indian mystic

That's why I love the Tibetan word for meditation: "familiarisation." It's not the practice of seeking anything new, it's the practice of discovering what is already here, beyond the seeking and judging and reacting mind.

You are that. You are that – you just need to stop and be it. Stop scaling a mountain of becoming, soak in the bath of being. As Nisargadatta Maharaj, the spiritual teacher, once said:

> *"There is not anything I can give you that you have not already got."*

The greatest of teachers can't actually give you anything. They can help you by reminding you of the truth of who you are, they certainly can remind you by being that presence themselves, but they can give you nothing beyond holding you in your perfection and letting you rise to that.

Giving Yourself Away

"If you want to give me something, give me your greed, your lusts, your weaknesses. That is what you really hold dear above all else. Give me everything that stands between you and God."

- Brahmananda Saraswati, Indian spiritual teacher

It can be the most frustrating of experiences *if* you think about it. I know I found it so, when I would get stuck into thinking about it – which I did, for years.

"How can I already be it, when I don't experience it all the time? When my mind keeps getting in the way? When I keep reacting in ways I regret? When I keep getting angry and depressed? When will I finally get it … ? What else do I have to *do* … ?" I would whine to Maharishi, my Bright Path Ishayas' Ascension teacher.

I was stuck in the search, in the attempt to become something else without actually doing the one thing that would take me beyond those parts of me and my life that I judged so much... being absolutely full of presence, now.

If you want to *do* something, fully give all your attention away.

Take your attention away from the selfish graspings of the mind, all the "shoulds," all the insisting, the living in the past and the future. Place it all on the still, silent presence that is beyond thought. There lies a field of quiet being, spacious... eternally patient.

The mind is constantly taking. It's nothing but "me, me, me" – and the world, through habit, is stuck in it. "Be someone" is the cry of the ego, the inner child: "but what about *me??*"

The small me has only brought you confusion and misery and searching for more. There have been periods of relative, temporary happiness and satisfaction for sure, but nothing lasting. The focus on what is wrong and the search for more takes over soon enough.

In comparison, that still silent, aware presence within wants, needs and takes nothing beyond simple appreciation. In giving your attention to it, you are quite literally giving away all your limitations and selfishness. You are returning yourself to Zero.

The more you do it, the more that becomes your ground of being; that lived sense of "I am that." In giving up the search, in fully tuning in to what this moment has to offer you, you step into living the greatest of lives.

The Not Doing Trap

"You may never know what results come from your action.
But if you do nothing, there will be no result."

- Mahatma Gandhi, Indian political and spiritual leader

Choosing peace and happiness doesn't mean choosing not to act. It doesn't mean choosing not to live.

Life is still about action, but it's about a different kind of action, one that is powered not by struggle and effort, but by Flow, inspiration and presence.

Early on in the book I talked a lot about how most of humanity lives blindly, automatically, reactively. Being Zero you also live a kind of automatic life, but one where your habits and programmes and filters don't affect your responses. You don't need to examine anything, you don't *want* to examine anything, you live freely as you are. Your choices come purely from your innate goodness and wisdom.

The struggle and strain and control disappears, that's why the little you "does" nothing.

It is impossible to describe, but get present, return to Zero and you will know it, you will live it.

It's not about inaction. Life isn't about waiting for things to be given to you. It's not about ignoring what you love to do, what you feel passionate about either. It's not about merely accepting everything as "perfect" and yet doing nothing when you feel called to do or say something.

Surrender to Zero isn't about zero action, zero desire, zero passion. Surrender is about getting out of the way of all the barriers that inhibit pure action, desire and passion.

Surrender is determining the difference between the mind and intuition. Again, don't think about this stuff, don't struggle with it, be presence itself and just go, see what happens.

The critical fact is you will return full circle. We started this book by saying one of the most important things you could have is innocence – having zero expectations or prejudice – about others, or indeed, yourself.

Innocence is what you are returned to, innocence is what will guide you.

Innocence

The whole world expects you to have an opinion, to be a part of something. "What do you believe in? Is this right? Is this wrong?"

When the whole world wants to divide and define according to belief and judgement, it is a pretty radical act to empty yourself and just be open, willing to understand and decide in the exact moment you need to understand and decide.

When the whole world wants you to stand for something, becoming Zero and rejoicing in the experience that there is no suffering now, that there is no problem in Presence, it all becomes clear:

You aren't your opinions, your beliefs, your culture. You aren't how you voted, your job, your possessions, what you have or haven't done. You aren't your dreams, you aren't your plans, you aren't your ideals.

You have these things, but they are not you.

If you think you are these things, then you also see others as these things. How can you connect with anyone purely, as they are? How can you truly understand anything when such prejudice clouds every interaction, every decision? How can you meet the exact needs of this moment – which is life itself?

You can't – not with these filters in play.

The only way to live cleanly is to drop all your beliefs, your expectations, your demands, your insistences. Then you can truly, truly be effective and filled with joy.

I'm not saying you give up your preferences and your passions. I'm not saying you don't care – but you care about reality, you flow with the clarity of what is rather than what your prejudiced mind, full of belief and opinion, says you should be.

Innocence is what we're talking about here. When you give the small you away, when you become Zero, you remember absolute innocence.

Innocence is not needing or resisting anything, but embracing everything that comes – it's the purest surrender and acceptance.

In innocence there is nothing left that is selfish or self-absorbed. Along with the loss of the limited mind comes losing the perspective of lack – the half-empty glass, and the resulting need to protect.

Instead, you live from a perspective of fullness, of abundance, of potential. Actually, the only perspective is fullness; no other possibility exists. You live superbly because you realise you never actually needed anything.

In innocence, you forget the demands that you place on yourself. You forget your ideas that you need to become something different and, in doing so, you forget the demands you place on everyone else.

There comes a fascination with what is, not with what you think should be. You expect nothing and celebrate everything.

In every interaction innocence is a great gift. Not assuming, not taking positions, just willing and wanting to interact and relate exactly to the person and not to your idea or agenda.

When you put down your masks and assumptions, you give everyone the freedom to do the same. You give everyone the space to be who they really are.

You can truly understand, you can truly see, you can truly act. You can truly transcend all suffering, the pain that comes from your own mind. You can truly make a difference: a force for unity, a force for purity of heart, mind, body and soul.

Don't Think About It

You can't think about returning to Zero, you can only do it. You cannot think your way to an experience.

Thoughts can label and comment on the experience, but it can never be the experience.

It is like the fish swimming in the ocean. The fish might be able to tell you what it thinks being wet is like, but from the ocean's point of view it knows nothing.

As my teacher Maharishi points out, it's the difference between thinking about chocolate and actually eating chocolate. Who wants to just think about it? And yet whole schools of philosophy, mindfulness and spiritual practice are founded on the thinking, on the theory.

Your focus on thinking will always prevent you from directly experiencing what is true, what is real, what is permanent. Thinking is the process that you mistakenly believe is you. You think you are your thoughts. You are not. You are the awareness that contains these thoughts, the empty fullness that they move through.

Beyond thinking, when you give away thinking – there You are. Don't think; be.

Now you may say, "If I am that, why do I need a practice? Why do I need anything at all?"

Because believing you are thought is such an ingrained habit (and a subtle one at that), having a practice, a tool to help let go and bring you back to the experience makes your complete return simple and swift.

You can wait for spontaneous awakening, to be hit by remembering lightning; or you can get going and get yourself a tool to help you return, now. You can be irregular with your choice, or you can fully find your way back home – the hard road or the easy road is up to you.

Return to Zero

"Enlightenment is the ego's ultimate disappointment."

- Chogyam Trungpa, Tibetan Buddhist teacher

Returning and remembering is the opposite of achieving and becoming. There are no awards, and when you return to Zero there's no part of you left to want the recognition that "you" achieved anything, anyway.

It is the opposite of the glamorous expectations of your mind. It is simple and natural, and because of this, it is "be-able" (not do-able) by you.

You will forget, you will fall asleep again. Forgetting doesn't matter, forgetting is irrelevant. Remembering is the only thing that counts; and you can only do that now.

Which part of you cares that you forgot? Which part of you is keeping score? The part of you that needs to become better. Zero doesn't care – it just loves having you home. Remembering and living it now is everything.

Again – you will forget. You will think about it. You will struggle and strain. You will do a host of things – but as many times you forget, simply remember without indulging in violent self-talk or recriminations.

Which part of you needs to destroy the ego? Which part of you needs to annihilate and destroy bad habits? Which part of you needs to punish and control?

Zero doesn't care that you forgot. The ocean has no concern with the fish, it has no opposition, it supports everything, it remains untouched by anything.

Hit the reset button and go again. Be fresh, open your eyes to what you now have, rather than what you didn't have a moment ago, or what you think you should have.

Live life based in the experience of Zero.

How are you going to know unless you do it? How are you going to know what it's like to be Zero if you don't engage the experience in the one moment you can – right now?

Just because no one else around you may be doing it, does it mean it's not True?

You already know it's true. You do – you just need to ignore the doubts of the mind – the one part of you that is actively invested in you not waking up to who you really are and the way you can really live your life.

If your mind kicks off about this, it is an excellent sign you're heading in the right direction. The very thing whose survival depends on you choosing for suffering and struggle and "me" is certain to try to distract you, to try to convince you that you're throwing everything away.

It will tell you that you won't like the "new you," but it's actually the only thing that doesn't love and accept you as you are now. It'll tell you all sorts of things to try and stay viable, to seem relevant to you.

All you have to do is ignore that voice, just now. You don't need to do it forever, just here and now – ignore it, engage the experience once again.

Keep doing that and the experience of the return to Zero means you won't want to stop. You don't stop and you become it. It gets so natural, it's hard to believe you could think that you were anything else, that you lived any other way.

What's more, all the choices I've detailed in this book? They are all fulfilled when you return to Zero.

Everything – a choice for peace, to own a conscious, accepting, appreciative, bold, loving, giving and present life is all contained within the one choice to be Zero.

That is the beauty and power of Zero – you *become* the choice; it's the natural expression, the natural attitude that living life inspires within you.

The biggest life possible is distilled from this one thing: get out of your own way; return.

"I have learned so much from God,
That I can no longer call myself
A Christian, a Hindu, a Muslim,
A Buddhist, a Jew.

The truth has shared so much of Itself with me,
That I can no longer call myself
A man, a woman, an angel,
Or even a pure soul.

Love has befriended Hafiz so completely,
It has turned to ash and freed me
Of every concept and image
My mind has ever known."

- Hafiz, Persian poet and mystic

CHAPTER SEVENTEEN

Living Fully – Truly Living

"When I stand before God at the end of my life,
I would hope that I would have not a single bit of talent
left and could say, 'I used everything you gave me'."

- Erma Bombeck, American author and newspaper columnist

The World Owes You Nothing

What a difference your attitude makes.

Some people live this life believing they deserve more. They are right – everyone continually deserves more – but theirs is a demand for more without appreciation of what they have, stomping their feet like a spoilt child, frustrated at how lacking they think their world is.

When you demand, ungrateful, the whole world turns its back on you.

The world does not owe you anything. On the contrary, you are absolutely blessed to be here.

Every moment that you are simply alive is nothing short of a miracle.

Realise that and you will be so filled with gratitude and awe you will never demand anything ever again.

You have so much, you are immersed in riches; why do you complain – about anything?

Choice

> "We who lived in concentration camps can remember the men who walked through the huts comforting others, giving away their last piece of bread. They may have been few in number, but they offer sufficient proof that everything can be taken from a man but one thing: the last of the human freedoms – to choose one's attitude in any given set of circumstances, to choose one's own way."
>
> - Viktor Frankl, Austrian neurologist, psychiatrist and Holocaust survivor

Your birthright is to know that it isn't life that brings you happiness, it is you that brings happiness to life. Consistently making this choice brings you beyond suffering and lack, forever.

Your life is your choice. No one else can choose for you.

Take full responsibility for your choices. And continually choose: fill your attention with acceptance, with what is good, with presence and aliveness, with Zero, and your life transforms.

It becomes simpler, more filled with Life, with purpose, with joyful clarity, ease and happiness. It becomes Ideal.

Here, now, nothing is lacking. Filled up, needing nothing, demanding for nothing, the whole world throws its treasure at you.

Imagine how would life be if you lived in a state of complete fulfilment, needing nothing but enjoying everything? How would life be if you *knew* peace or pain was your choice, and choosing for peace was as simple as remembering?

Keeping Important Things Important

Keep as the foundation of your life your highest desire, that thing that is truly most important to you, always.

Make that the core of any solution to any problem or situation.

No matter what you do – in everything you do – have your priority as peace and happiness and love.

It doesn't mean don't take action, but don't lose sight of what is most important to you. Otherwise you lose everything.

Don't lose yourself in the circumstances of life, even when the circumstances of life appear important, crucial even.

Always hold the important things as truly important, and don't let seemingly urgent things take precedence instead.

To do so, it can help to treat life like a game.

Play to win, but know it is a game. Seriousness only comes in when you could win or lose. Play well and play fully, but the fact is that in the great game of life the only time you lose is when you forget your connection with what is truly of the highest importance to you.

And so, keep peace and happiness and love as a priority in all things, have a smile and a light heart, and see what happens from there.

The right course of action always reveals itself from this foundation.

It's mastery in action so don't worry if you forget. You will get better at remembering. The only thing that is truly important is that you remember in this moment.

Just remember.

The Truth Is ...

Time is short: You are dying; day by day, moment by moment.

You may not know this. So many people live in a dream, unaware, assuming there will always be more time. But as each moment goes by, there is less time.

You have no time to waste, delaying what is important to you. There may not be a later. You don't know how long your life will be.

When I was younger, I had quite a few friends die. Being in a community involved in outdoor adventure sports, people got hurt and sometimes died. Others committed suicide. One got cancer. One was hit by a car cycling down the road.

What all those funerals for people under 30 showed me was I'd better get my priorities lined up and fully live before I too ran out of time. It wasn't easy to experience, but I'm glad that I did.

Unless you're aware, you will waste your life with dreams undone and words unsaid. I was given the gift of being shown this early on. Many aren't. But the lesson is there for everyone: don't waste your life. Every moment counts, live each one fully.

Truly Living? Or Dying Slowly?

"When you were born, you cried and the world rejoiced.
Live your life so that when you die, the world cries and you rejoice."

- Anon

At the end of the movie *Saving Private Ryan*, Private Ryan, now in old age, goes to visit the graves of the men who died rescuing him.

He breaks down in tears. "Tell me I've lived a good life," he asks his wife.

He wants recognition that his life has been worthwhile. He's saying that he knows he was given the chance to live by men who died, and he wants to know that he made the most of it.

The scene touched me on so many levels. What it boils down to is this: I don't want to get to the end of my life and not be sure. Or worse, I don't want to get to the end and know that I missed something through fear or laziness.

Death is a big prompt for many to question what life is all about. Typically, the mind also comes fully to the fore with regret for things said and unsaid, done and undone.

Living a rich, meaningful life for me is living without regret – becoming

Zero and experiencing the full Truth of life so that regret has no hold on this moment; at the same time doing all that I can to fully play my role in each and every moment, to make sure no seeds of regret are sown.

The real beauty of knowing the truth is that each moment can die cleanly, leaving no trace, so that this moment can be truly lived, fresh and new.

"Is there life before death? That is the question!"

- Anthony de Mello, Jesuit priest and spiritual teacher

Don't Delay

"If you don't break your ropes while you are alive,
do you think ghosts will do it after?"

- Kabir, Indian poet and mystic

Don't delay your choice for peace, for awareness. Seek it within; seek it now.

If this book contains something that is of interest to you, then follow it through. Practise what it says. If you are interested, learn the Bright Path Ishayas' Ascension; it is worth its weight in gold.

But make being the best version of yourself a priority – don't accept excuses from your mind. You now have the ability and knowledge to transform your life; it's just a matter of doing it.

My teacher Maharishi Krishnananda once said that any one of us can experience all the wonders of the world – the wonders that sages have talked about for millennia:

"It's never a case of 'Can you?', but 'Will you?'"

You could choose to ignore all of this. You could toss this book aside, thinking "I'm alright. Life is pretty good. I'm okay settling for less." But as psychologist Abraham Maslow cautions:

> *"If you deliberately plan on being less than you are capable of being,*
> *then I warn you that you'll be unhappy for the rest of your life."*

You don't want to get to the end of your life only half-lived as some compromised version of yourself. The chance to be fully alive, fully focused, fully calm, clear and content – to live a life of 200% – is on the table, and it's all your choice. It's all up to you.

What if it was real? What if everything the sages say is true? Would you go for it?

What if?

And if not now, when?

"It is a blessing to be granted a desire to be free.

*It is an immense blessing to have that spark of desire to experience
something more than what we were told life should be.*

*It is a blessing to have the desire to experience everything
in its fullest rather than trying to survive.*

*It is a great blessing to really want to know who we truly
are beyond who we think we have been.*

*And, it is one thing to recognise that desire, it is another thing to make
that desire your priority, it is up to us to make it such a burning
desire that we create exactly what we need to achieve it.*

*And people who actually follow the call of that desire and find their
path are even a lot fewer. But it is by choice."*

- Maharishi Krishnananda Ishaya, Bright Path Ishaya teacher

The Bright Path

In writing this book I found many very cool quotes that said everything I wanted to say, only in fewer, sweeter words. It became obvious that there were people living thousands of years ago who embodied everything that I wanted to say in this book. Ha!

There's nothing new under the sun. When it comes to the truth this is totally true. The truth of everyone's heart is the same. Whether they recognise it or not is the crucial thing.

When you experience the underlying truth of existence your words may differ, but it is the same experience, the universal experience at the heart of everyone's soul.

No culture, no religion, no person has a hold over the truth. All these things are just sign-posts at best.

The question is really, what speaks to your heart? What helps you remember?

For me, that is the practice of the Bright Path Ishayas' Ascension. You may have noticed how high in my esteem it is, and I wanted to say a few more things about it.

It is what I practise and love to teach above all things. I can't think of anything else that I would recommend more strongly to anyone.

And I know I'm biased, but I like to think that I have a smidgen of credibility and objectivity left within me.

This is not the next great thing in a long list of great things, only to be replaced by something shinier next week; I believe this is *the* magic stuff right here.

I've been practising and teaching since 2003 and I continuously get so much from it. If it didn't work completely for anyone who practises it, not least of all myself, I would be off looking for something else.

It says a lot that I'm not.

The practice brings peace, clarity, purpose and simplicity. Focus, fun, fluidity. It does it all so easily – a set of tools you use to fit into your life, so you can get the most out of your life.

The teachers will support you as much as you want and need. The community of Ascenders is international, and alive.

I do apologise if, in my eagerness, I have come across as a little evangelical about Ascension. My intention is never ever to say, "This is the way, the only way, do or die." I do believe in freedom of informed, aware choice over all things.

My intention is rather to express the profound value of this simple practice in living a great life completely free from suffering. You can gain so much by doing so little.

So there you have it: I wish you nothing but fulfilment no matter what path you take or choices you make, whether you learn Ascension or not.

Honestly – may you have the best life possible.

If you ever need anything or have any questions, please don't hesitate to get in touch. I'd love to help.

The Bright Path website is: www.thebrightpath.com.

If you visit www.arjunaishaya.com/freestuff, you can download some helpful guides and get on my email list. It would be great to have you.

If you're interested in working closely with me in transforming your relationship with your mind and living 200% of life, then see www.arjunaishaya.com/mentoring for more details.

ABOUT THE AUTHOR

I'm from New Zealand but now live in North Yorkshire, UK. I was travelling the world teaching the Bright Path Ishayas' Ascension meditation when I met a girl. It got serious and, as you do, we settled down to have a family in her home town.

I love the outdoors. I used to be an outdoor instructor because I loved it and I loved helping people. I still get out kayaking and into the hills as much as I can.

I love travelling and I love eating. If I had a million gold pieces I would spend them all on taking my family and buddies around the world. We'd go on some outdoor mission to gather up a big hunger and then all meet up for a fine meal and even better conversation.

I love writing, good books and movies too.

Life is good, really good. I don't just say that in a Facebook/Instagram glossing over the cracks way of trying to make myself feel better or seem better than anyone else, but honestly, truly: life is good.

It makes sense now, where it didn't always. I know how it works. I know how to have aliveness and connection and meaning, I know how to fully enjoy each and every moment, I know how to live as the ever-evolving best version of me.

As I said, it wasn't always this way. I bumbled along for years, half-wondering if there was more to life than what I was living (but not looking that hard, because it all seemed pretty good), when I fell into a bit of a dark hole. Then the search for more really began in earnest. Getting a little stuck and confused seemed to be just the thing I needed because it led me straight to being a Bright Path Ishaya monk and meditation teacher in 2003. Then life started to really come together, and quickly.

Today, I love teaching and sharing what I've discovered and continue to discover. I love making it as simple and clear as possible: practical and applicable to "real" women and men's lives.

Life is good.

Onwards!

BIBLIOGRAPHY & NOTES

A big chunk of the quotes I've used in this book have come from notebooks that I used to carry with me. For years they served as a kind of treasure map, pointing me at the Truth, reminding me where to look, cajoling me to live the life I really wanted to live. Just as if they were a real-life pirate treasure map, these notebooks were one of my most important possessions for quite some time. Now, I still love a good quote – and as wonderful as external reminders still are – I am so grateful I no longer *need* them to remember.

But at the time of scribbling down something that truly illuminated or provoked me, I wasn't very interested in the complete details. Which, now that I want to properly acknowledge all the authors and sources, would have been a great idea. If I've messed up in attributing something of yours, I'm sorry – let me know and I'll fix it. Thank you!

Front papers

"Be whole-assed ..."
Maharishi Krishnananda Ishaya, A favourite saying of his

"Nothing of me is ..."
Chuck Palahniuk, *Invisible Monsters* (Vintage, 2000)

"There is more to ..."
Mahatma Gandhi, attributed

"It is not death that ..."
Marcus Aurelius, George Long (Trans.), *Meditations*.
Available at: http://classics.mit.edu/Antoninus/meditations.html

"Simplicity is the ..."
Leonardo da Vinci, attributed

Chapter One

"A tennis player first ..."
Tim Gallwey, *The Inner Game of Tennis: The Ultimate Guide to The Mental Side Of Peak Performance* (Random House, 1974)

Great leaders ...
Jim Collins, *Good to Great: Why Some Companies Make The Leap ... and Others Don't* (HarperBusiness, 2005)

"We treat rest as ..."
Paul Mort, from an online seminar in 2017. See:
https://unstoppablemanproject.com

"Sometimes the most ..."
Ashleigh Brilliant. For more of his great work see:
www.ashleighbrilliant.com

Chapter Two

"Everything has been figured ..."
Jean Paul Sartre, attributed

"Hell is other people ..."
Jean Paul Sartre, from his play *No Exit*

Chapter Three

"There is ultimately only …"
Kim Christie, a beautiful post from her personal Facebook page. I've now lost the source. Sorry Kim!

Chapter Four

"Oh, I don't really think …"
Diane Piper, quoted in Kira Cochrane, "Katie Piper: I asked mum to kill me," *The Guardian*, 2 June 2012.
Available at: https://www.theguardian.com/lifeandstyle/2012/jun/02/katie-piper-acid-attack-book

Katie Piper
For more about Katie's work, see:
https://katiepiperfoundation.org.uk

"We are what we …"
Aristotle, attributed

"There are only two …"
Buddha, attributed

Chapter Five

"If you don't know …"
Chuck Palahniuk, *Fight Club* (Vintage, 1997)

Chapter Seven

"Not having enough time …"
Priya Ishaya, unpublished writing

"I have two kinds ..."

Dwight Eisenhower, from an address at the Second Assembly of the World Council of Churches, Evanston, Illinois, 19 August 1954.

Available at: http://www.presidency.ucsb.edu/ws/?pid=9991

"Our outer world reflects ..."

Debbie Ford, *The Right Questions: Ten Essential Questions to Guide You to an Extraordinary Life* (Bravo, 2004)

"If it's important ..."

Dan John, "The Gable Method," *T-Nation* 15 June 2006.

Available at: https://www.t-nation.com/training/gable-method

"A journey of a ..."

Lao Tsu, *Tao Te Ching*.

Available at: http://thetaoteching.com/taoteching44.html

"We do not see ..."

The Talmud, attributed

"Have strong opinions ..."

Philip Goldman, personal communication circa 2012

"Laugh at what you ..."

Abraham Maslow, quoted in Loretta LaRoche, *Relax — You May Have Only a Few Minutes Left : Using the Power of Humor to Overcome Stress in Your Life and Work* (Hay House, 1998)

"Sacred cows make the ..."

Mark Twain, attributed

Chapter Eight

"Give me the ..."

Alcoholics Anonymous, The Serenity Prayer is the common name for a prayer written by the American theologian Reinhold Niebuhr

"The only true failure ..."

Pat Flynn, from his email list and blog.

Available at: www.chroniclesofstrength.com. I have lost the original email. Sorry Pat.

Chapter Nine

"Nothing surpasses the holiness ..."

Anthony de Mello, *Taking Flight: A Book of Story Meditations* (Image, 1990)

Chapter Ten

"Any remaining emotional response ..."

Jill Bolte Taylor, *My Stroke of Insight: A Brain Scientist's Personal Journey* (Hodder, 2009)

"The animals feel secure ..."

Dax Moy, from an online seminar in 2017. See http://www.mindmapcoach.com for more about his work.

The online seminar is available when you opt in for his free report, here: http://www.mindmapcoach.com/mindmap-mapped-2018/
Well worth watching if you're interested in how the brain can shape behaviour

Chapter Eleven

"Accept – then act ..."

Eckhart Tolle, *The Power of Now: A Guide to Spiritual Enlightenment* (Yellow Kite, 2001)

"Happiness and freedom begin ..."

Epictetus, with Sharon Lebell, *Art of Living: The Classical Manual on Virtue, Happiness, and Effectiveness* (HarperOne, 2007)

"Now I take nothing for ..."
Lance Armstrong, attributed

Chapter Twelve

"Men are disturbed not ..."
Epictetus, George Long (Trans.), *Selections from the Discourses of Epictetus, with the Encheiridion* (Leopold Classic Library, 2016)

"I never doubted ..." and "This is a very ..."
James Stockdale, quoted in Jim Collins, *Good to Great: Why Some Companies Make The Leap ... and Others Don't* (HarperBusiness, 2005)

"What can everyone do? ..."
Friedrich Nietzsche, attributed, possibly from *Sämtliche Werke: Kritische Studienausgabe* (Walter de Gruyter, 1980) - for details see:
https://www.poemhunter.com/quotations/famous.asp?people=Friedrich%20Nietzsche&p=75

"Gratitude unlocks the fullness ..."
Melody Beattie, *The Language of Letting Go: Daily Meditations on Codependency* (Hazelden FIRM, 1990)

"It may sound absolutely ..."
Martine Wright, quoted in Sue Mott, "7/7 bombings 10 years on: Martine Wright lost both legs in the attack – she explains how her experience since shows 'anything is possible'," *The Independent*, 27 June 2015.
Available at: https://www.independent.co.uk/news/uk/home-news/77-bombings-10-years-on-martine-wright-lost-both-legs-in-the-attack-she-explains-how-her-experience-10350219.html

Martine Wright's book
Martine Wright, *Unbroken: My Story of Survival From 7/7 Bombings to Paralympic Success* (Simon & Schuster UK, 2017)

"The future gap ..." and "list of wins ..."
Paul Mort, from an online seminar in 2017.
See https://unstoppablemanproject.com

"Be content in what ..."
Lao Tzu, *Tao Te Ching*.
Available at: http://thetaoteching.com/taoteching44.html

"What the caterpillar calls ..."
Richard Bach, *Illusions: The Adventures of a Reluctant Messiah* (Dell Publishing Company, 1989)

"If you want to awaken ..."
Wang Fou, *Hua Hu Ching*. Quoted in Ian Chadwick, "Bad Lao Tzu meme adds to growing list of mis-identified quotes online," *Scripturient*, 7 February 2012.
Available at: http://ianchadwick.com/blog/bad-lao-tzu-meme-adds-to-growing-list-of-mis-identified-quotes-online/

"We are not here ..."
Anthony de Mello, *Awareness* (Zondervan, 1990)

"No problem can be ..."
Albert Einstein, attributed

"The simple guiding principle ..."
Maharishi Sadashiva Isham, *Ascension: Analysis of the Art of Ascension as Taught by the Ishayas* (Society for Ascension UK, 1991)

"Judge not, lest you ..."
Jesus, *Matthew 7:1*
Available at: https://www.bible.com

"Don't change: Desire to ..."
Anthony de Mello, Quoted in Carlos G Valles, *Unencumbered By Baggage: Tony De Mello, a Prophet for Our Times* (Gujarat Sahitya Prakash, 1987)

"To be beautiful means ..."
Thich Nhat Hanh, The Art of Power (HarperOne, 2008)

Successful relationship ratio ...
John Gottman, *What Predicts Divorce?* quoted in Ellie Lisitsa, "The Workplace: The Ideal Praise-to-Criticism Ratio," *The Gottman Institute* website, 3 April 2013.

The research detailing the 5:1 ratio appearing in successful teams of people is quoted in the same article.
Available here: https://www.gottman.com/blog/the-workplace-the-ideal-praise-to-criticism-ratio/

"Now, Kalamas, don't go ..."
Buddha, *Kalama Sutta*. Available at:
https://www.accesstoinsight.org/tipitaka/an/an03/an03.065.than.html

Chapter Thirteen

"If you knew what I ..."
Buddha, quoted in Jack Kornfield and Joseph Goldstein, *Seeking the Heart of Wisdom: The Path of Insight Meditation* (Shambhala, 2001)

"You give but little ..."
Kahlil Gibran, *The Prophet* (BN Publishing, 2009)

"Wise are those who ..."
Maharishi Sadashiva Isham, unpublished collection of writings

"Be the change you ..."
Mahatma Gandhi, attributed

"For it is in giving ..."
St. Francis of Assisi, *The Prayer of St. Francis.*
Available at: https://www.crosswalk.com/faith/prayer/prayers/the-prayer-of-st-francis-make-me-an-instrument.html

"Do to others ..."
Jesus, *Luke 6:31*
Available at: https://www.bible.com

"Treat people as if they ..."
Johann Wolfgang von Goethe, attributed

"Money is like love ..."
Kahlil Gibran, quoted in Neil Douglas-Klotz, *Kahlil Gibran's Little Book of Life* (Hampton Roads Publishing, 2018)

Chapter Fourteen

"Many people are alive ..."
Thich Nhat Hanh, *The Miracle Of Mindfulness: The Classic Guide to Meditation by the World's Most Revered Master* (Rider, 2008)

"Life is what happens ..."
John Lennon, attributed

"Most people treat the ..."
Eckhart Tolle, quoted in Kathy Juline, "Awakening to Your Life's Purpose," *Science of Mind* Magazine.
Available at: https://www.eckharttolletv.com/article/Awakening-Your-Spiritual-Lifes-Purpose/

"If you get the inside ..."
Eckhart Tolle, *The Power of Now: A Guide to Spiritual Enlightenment* (Yellow Kite, 2001)

"The worst bullies you ..."
Bryant McGill, *Simple Reminders: Inspiration for Living Your Best Life* (SRN Publishing, 2015)

"Thought can organize the ..."
Anthony de Mello, *One Minute Wisdom* (Bantam Doubleday Dell, 1985)

"We are what we think ..."
Buddha, quoted in Thomas Byrom, *The Dhammapada: The Sayings of the Buddha* (Vintage, 2011)

"The aim of life is …"
Henry Miller, *Tropic of Capricorn* (Penguin Classics, 2015)

"The affairs of the world …"
Milarepa, quoted in Garma C.C. Chang (Ed.), *The Hundred Thousand Songs of Milarepa* (Shambhala, 1977)

"What we plant in the …"
Meister Eckhart, quoted in Richard Alan Krieger, *Civilization's Quotations: Life's Ideal* (Algora, 2002)

"You can never embarrass …"
Jeff Brown, attributed. I wrote this down a long time ago and cannot find the original source. I even wrote to Jeff – he replied that it sounded like something he could have written, but he didn't think it was something from one of his books. So if you wrote it, let me know!

"When you're going through …"
Winston Churchill, attributed

"Wherever you are …"
Matt Haig, *Reasons To Stay Alive* (Canongate, 2015)

"Difficulty shows what men …"
Epictetus, W. A. Oldfather (Trans.), *Discourses* (Loeb, 1989)

Chapter Fifteen

"I've never seen any …"
Elizabeth Gilbert, from her website, 7 May 2014.
Available at: https://www.elizabethgilbert.com/dear-ones-yesterday-i-wrote-on-twitter-ive-never-seen-any-life-transformati/

"It is better to conquer …"
Buddha, quoted in Thomas Byrom, *The Dhammapada: The Sayings of the Buddha* (Vintage, 2011)

"I don't believe people ..."

Joseph Campbell, *The Power of Myth* (Anchor, 1991)

"Follow your bliss ..."

Joseph Campbell, *The Power of Myth* (Anchor, 1991)

"To invent your own ..."

Bill Watterson, from a speech given at Kenyon College, Ohio, to the 1990 graduating class.

Available at: http://web.mit.edu/jmorzins/www/C-H-speech.html

"Don't ask what the world ..."

Harold Thurman, quoted in Gil Bailie, *Violence Unveiled: Humanity at the Crossroads* (Crossroad Publishing, 1996)

"Take action. Every story ..."

Bradley Whitford, from a commencement address given at the University of Wisconsin–Madison, to the 2004 graduating class.

Available at: https://news.wisc.edu/spring-commencement-transcript-of-address-by-bradley-whitford/

"Are you paralyzed with ..."

Steven Pressfield, *The War of Art: Break Through the Blocks and Win Your Inner Creative Battles* (Black Irish Entertainment, 2012)

"Whenever there is fear ..."

Osho, *Emotional Wellness: Transforming Fear, Anger, and Jealousy into Creative Energy* (Harmony Books, 2007)

"Courage is not the ..."

Ambrose Redmoon, quoted in Julia Keller, "The mysterious Ambrose Redmoon's healing words," *Chicago Tribune*, 29 March 2002.

Available at: http://articles.chicagotribune.com/2002-03-29/features/0203290018_1_chicago-police-officer-terry-hillard-courage

"The price of inaction ..."

Meister Eckhart, quoted in James Geary, *Geary's Guide to the World's Great Aphorists* (Bloomsbury, 2007)

Reframing mistakes tool …
Paul Mort, from an online seminar in 2017.
See https://unstoppablemanproject.com

"The only true failure …"
Pat Flynn, from his email and blog.
Available at: www.chroniclesofstrength.com. Again, I lost the original email.

"All you have to do …"
Maharishi Sadashiva Isham, unpublished collection of writings

"If you want to improve …"
Epictetus, Elizabeth Carter (Trans.), *The Enchiridion*.
Available at: http://classics.mit.edu/Epictetus/epicench.html

"You are the only problem …"
Bob Proctor, from his Facebook page, 4 November 2012.
Available at: https://www.facebook.com/OfficialBobProctor/posts/you-are-the-only-problem-you-will-ever-have-and-you-are-the-only-solution-change/10151235359999421/

"Whether you think you …"
Henry Ford, attributed

"Life is meant to be lived …"
Maharishi Sadashiva Isham, "Unity," *The Ascending Current*, Society for Ascension newsletter, date lost

"Since death is inevitable …"
Nisargadatta Maharaj, *The Lost Satsang*.
Video available at: https://www.youtube.com/watch?v=ejDUEW9xdSQ.

Success process and "If I learned one lesson …"
Dan John, "Show Up, Don't Quit, Ask Questions," from his blog.
Available at: http://danjohn.net/100reps/

"It takes courage to …"
Priya Ishaya, unpublished writing

"The curious paradox is ..."

Carl Rogers, *On Becoming a Person: A Therapist's View of Psychotherapy* (Mariner Books, 1995)

"Once you realize that ..."

Nisargadatta Maharaj, *I am That: Talks with Sri Nisargadatta Maharaj* (Chetana Private, 1999)

Chapter Sixteen

"When you make yourself ..."

Mahatma Gandhi, attributed – because I can't find the source. Though he often said or wrote, "I must reduce myself to zero." He also said, "If you would swim on the bosom of the ocean of Truth, you must reduce yourself to zero," which I love. Quoted in Homer A. Jack (Ed.), *The Wit and Wisdom of Gandhi* (Dover, 2005)

"God is not found in ..."

Meister Eckhart, quoted in Matthew Fox, *Meister Eckhart: A Mystic-Warrior for Our Times* (New World Library, 2014)

"The Universe is saying ..."

Klaus Joehle, attributed

"All spiritual teachings are ..."

Ramana Maharishi, quoted in Matthew Greenblatt, *The Essential Teachings of Ramana Maharshi: A Visual Journey* (Inner Directions Publishing, 2001)

"There is not anything ..."

Nisargadatta Maharaj, attributed

"If you want to give ..."

Brahmananda Saraswati, I've lost the original source, but it's similar to: "If you have to make an offering, offer not your money but your defects, so that you are redeemed and made whole," which is quoted by Paul Mason in *The Teachings of Guru Dev - The Roots of TM. Quotations of Shankaracharya Swami Brahmananda Saraswati.*

Available at: http://www.paulmason.info/gurudev/miscellaneous.htm

"You may never know ..."
Mahatma Gandhi, attributed

"Enlightenment is the ego's ..."
Chogyam Trungpa, quoted in Jun Po Denis Kelly Roshi and Keith Martin-Smith, *The Heart of Zen: Enlightenment, Emotional Maturity, and What It Really Takes for Spiritual Liberation* (North Atlantic Books, 2014)

"I have learned so ..."
Hafiz, Daniel Ladinsky (Trans.), *The Gift: Poems by Hafiz, the Great Sufi Master* (Penguin Books, 1999)

Chapter Seventeen

"When I stand before ..."
Erma Bombeck, attributed

"We who lived in ..."
Viktor Frankl, *Man's Search For Meaning: The classic tribute to hope from the Holocaust* (Rider, 2004)

"Is there life before ..."
Anthony de Mello, *One Minute Wisdom* (Bantam Doubleday Dell, 1985)

"If you don't break ..."
Kabir, quoted in Jon Kabat-Zinn, *Meditation is Not What You Think: Mindfulness and Why It Is So Important* (Piatkus, 2018)

"It's never a case of ..."
Maharishi Krishnananda Ishaya, from a talk given in Spain, 2015

"If you plan on being ..."
Abraham Maslow, quoted in Joan Neehall-Davidson, *Perfecting Your Private Practice: Suggestions and Strategies for Psychologists* (Trafford Publishing, 2004)

"It is a blessing to ..."
Maharishi Krishnananda Ishaya, unpublished writing

Printed in Poland
by Amazon Fulfillment
Poland Sp. z o.o., Wrocław